Love Happiness

Factors associated with long-term empathic love

Vincenzo Berghella

Copyright Page

Copyright year: 2024

ISBN No: 979-8-218-32243-4

From the same author: (see also www.lulu.com)

1. **Obstetric Evidence Based Guidelines.** Informa Healthcare, London, UK, and New York, USA (2007) [English]

2. **Maternal Fetal Evidence Based Guidelines.** Informa Healthcare, London, UK, and New York, USA (2007) [English]

3. **Laughter, the best medicine.** Jokes for everyone. (2007) [English]

4. **Ridere, la migliore medicina. Barzellette per bambini.** (2007) [Italiano]

5. **My favorite quotes.** (2009) [English]

6. **In medio stat virtus – Citazioni d'autore.** (2009) [Italiano]

7. **Quello che di voi vive in me.** (2009) [Italiano]

8. **Dall'altra parte dell'oceano.** (2010) [Italiano] [Translated in: **On the other side of the ocean.** (2013) [English]

9. **Preterm Birth: Prevention and Management.** Wiley-Blackwell. Oxford, United Kingdom. (2010) [English]

10. **From father to son.** (2010) [English]

11. **Sollazzi.** (2010) [Italiano]

12. **The land of religions.** (2011) [English] [Translated in: **La terra delle religioni.** (2013) [Italiano]

13. **Giramondo.** (2011) [Italiano]

14. **Obstetric Evidence Based Guidelines.** Informa Healthcare, London, UK, and New York, USA (2012; Second Edition) [English]

15. **Maternal Fetal Evidence Based Guidelines.** Informa Healthcare, London, UK, and New York, USA (2012; Second Edition) [English]

16. **Trip to London.** (2012) [English]

17. **Il primo amore non si scorda mai.** (2012) [Italiano]

18. **Maldives.** (2013) [English]

19. **Russia.** (2013) [English]

20. **Happiness: the scientific path to achieving wellbeing.** (2014) [English] (Translated in **Felicita': il percorso scientifico per raggiungere il benessere.** [Italian])

21. **New Zealand: 100% pure.** (2014) [English]

22. **Me dentro: i primi scritti dai 17 ai 20 anni.** (2015) [Italiano]

23. **Me dentro: alla ricerca dell'amore.** (2015) [Italiano]

24. **US Rowing Youth Nationals.** (2015) [English]

25. **Polynesia.** (2016) [English]

26. **Obstetrics: Normal and Problem Pregnancies.** Gabbe, Niebyl, Simpson, Landon, Galan, Jauniaux, Driscoll, Berghella, Grobman. Elsevier, Philadelphia, USA (2016; Seventh Edition) [English]

27. **Obstetric Evidence Based Guidelines.** CRC Press, London, UK, and New York, USA (2017; Third Edition) [English]

28. **Maternal Fetal Evidence Based Guidelines.** CRC Press, London, UK, and New York, USA (2017; Third Edition) [English]

29. **Operative Obstetrics.** Apuzzio, Vintzileos, Berghella, Alvarez-Perez. CRC Press, London, UK, and New York, USA (2017; Fourth Edition) [English]

30. **Krakow and Auschwitz.** (2017) [English]

31. **Barcelona lo tiene todo.** (2017) [English]

32. **Chennai and Coimbatore, India.** (2018) [English]

33. **M'zav, Algeria.** (2018) [English]

34. **Labor and Delivery: Evidence Based Management.** (Berghella, Saccone, Ghi, Roman) JayPee Brothers, India (2018) [English]

35. **Gabbe's Obstetrics Essentials: Normal & Problem Pregnancies.** Landon, Driscoll, Jauniaux, Galan, Grobman, Berghella. (2018, 1st Edition) [English]

36. **Good Practice and Malpractice in Labor and Delivery.** Di Renzo, Berghella, Malvasi. (2019) [English]

37. **New Technologies and Perinatal Medicine: Prediction and Prevention of Pregnancy Complications.** Hod, Berghella, D'Alton, Di Renzo, Gratacos, Fanos. (2019) [English]

38. **Obstetrics: Normal and Problem Pregnancies.** Kilpatrick, Cahill, Landon, Galan, Jauniaux, Driscoll, Berghella, Grobman. Elsevier, Philadelphia, USA (2020; Eight Edition) [English]

39. **Obstetric Evidence Based Guidelines.** CRC Press, London, UK, and New York, USA (2022; Fourth Edition) [English]

40. **Maternal Fetal Evidence Based Guidelines.** CRC Press, London, UK, and New York, USA (2022; Fourth Edition) [English]

Index

I dedicate this book to my children Andrea, Pietro, Cesare, and Giulia, in the hope they will have happy love relationships.

I thank my wife Federica for letting my lifelong dream of living for true love come true, and for being so inspirational for me in writing this book with conviction and passion.

*Love, Giovinda, seems to me **the most important issue**. I leave to the great philosophers to understand the world, to explain it, to despise it. I only care to love the world, not to despise it, not to hate it and to hate me; I only care to **consider the world, with all beings, with love, admiration and respect**...*

                                 Herman Hesse, in 'Siddharta'

Introduction

People think love is an emotion. Love is good sense.
Ken Kersey

Love does not have a why; it is the why.
Massimo Gramellini

The success at loving someone and being loved back by this partner is the experience that will have the most impact on our happiness and our health. In the end, **you will measure your success in life by the strength of the bond you have achieved with your loved one.** This book is the **summary of the science on what to do to achieve love happiness.**

There are two human universals: that we are all born helpless and dependent, and that we are all mortals. The only way we have to best deal with this vulnerability, is to reach out and hold for another human being. First our mother, our father. Then, calmed and strengthened by this early love, we can do everything we want in life. And as adults, the new and long-term loving attachment should be our love partner.

"Whatever love means": this is, sadly, what King Charles III, then the Prince of Wales and married to Princess Diana, said, negatively and pessimistically, when asked about his relationship with Lady D. **Love is not a mystery at all.** We actually know what love means, and what love is. Love is well studied, logical, scientific, understandable, and achievable by most.

"**I want to live for love.**" This is what I wrote in my diary when I was 17 years old. I actually wrote "Voglio vivere per l'amore," since then all I spoke and wrote was my native Italian. After 40 more years of yearning for love, searching for love, living love, achieving love, I feel ready to share some tips on how to be happy in love.

There is no other life experience that has more impact in our lives than our success at loving and being loved. Research shows relationships, in particular the one with your love partner, are the number one key to achieving happiness.[1] **We feel safe and strong when we are sure we can love and we are reciprocated.** The comfort of our loved one

1

is what keeps us going in good and especially in bad times. Stable loving romantic relationships are scientifically proven to be the cornerstone of human happiness and well-being.

I called this book **Love happiness**, as there are many interpretations of love, and mine is linked to happiness. And linked to science. In my prior book 'Happiness: the scientific path to achieving well-being,'[1] I provided scientific proof that **the six activities which create happiness** are:

- Social relationships
- Doing what you like to do
- Having goals
- Finding a greater meaning
- Working hard
- Recognition

Love happiness is linked to these principles. **Romantic love between two persons**, which is the focus of this book, is the **ultimate social relationship**. The overwhelming scientific evidence is that **healthy, positive, close social relationships are the #1 key to achieving happiness. The romantic love relationship between two persons is the crucial deepest most meaningful social interaction**.

In this book, we'll explore how, like happiness, **romantic love with another person does not come to us freely**. Love must be something we like, something we desire to achieve as a goal, something we believe will give greater meaning to our life.

Long-term empathic love will **require our most commitment and labor** for it to be successful. Ultimately this effort will **result in not only loving another human being with all of ourselves, but also being loved back and appreciated by our partner.**

In the US, about half of marriages end up in divorce, and about half of partners in domestic relationships cheat on their partners. The data show that only a small minority of couples are in a happy love relationships; percentages are hard to come by, but probably only less than 10% of couples are truly happy on both partners' sides. Studies though do show **the thrill can last forever**. So what do these couples do that others don't? What are the secrets?

'Love is the secret,' many people say. I'm hoping it does not continue to be a secret. I wrote this book for you, and for me. Just like I follow the evidence on how to be happy as written in my 'Happiness' book,[1] I'm going to follow for the rest of my life the principles written in this book on how to achieve love happiness, and spread this guidance to as many people as I can. You can get love happiness if you follow this guidance, and work hard at the values I'll describe. Love is actually logical and understandable. It is not a secret at all!

The recommendations made in this book are based on scientific studies. Like for my many (>10) medical textbooks, my many (>600) peer-reviewed scientific articles, I searched for scientific data, for human experiments, for the best level 1 evidence. I read voraciously about the subject of romantic love for over 40 years. This book is the fruit of decades of study notes.

This book is mostly focused on **prevention,** rather than cure. Like I do as a physician and an educator, I prefer to prevent an unhappy love relationship in the first place. There are innumerous books about how to try to repair or escape from a bad relationship. This one covers that, but it **mostly helps to choose the right mate in the first place, and them teaches us how to behave to stay love happy for the long-term.**

This book **concentrates on empathic, mature, long-term love.** Falling in love is easy. I cover not only falling in love with the right person, but as importantly **staying in love for a lifetime.** Finding altruistic, reciprocal, unconditional love for each other. There is too much emphasis on Passionate Love. What about Empathic Love? How do you stay happily together for decades?

I am disappointed at the fact that today's society, in media, movies and everywhere, depicts mostly passionate love, and not long-term empathic love. Young people beginning to enter romantic relationships have no idea about what the keys to successful long-term relationships are. In fact, they are bombarded about short term passionate sex, and about the boredom and gloom of long-term relationships. It should not be that way, because many, albeit a small minority, have found love happiness in long-term empathic love. This book wants to fill this void and describe the keys to achieving lasting love happiness with your partner.

3

This book also **concentrates on the positive side**, on the good, rather than on the struggle, the bad. It starts from the optimistic act of falling in love, and provides the cookbook for keeping the love flame burning for a long time. The approach is that of Positive Psychology. I won't concentrate on failing or failed relationship, but on how to build and keep a successful one. Just like Positive Psychology does not dwell much on depression, but on how to stay happy and look at the glass half full.

Long-term love is a lot of work, and worth the effort. You will need to be a superhero and take action over and over again to get to the promised land of empathic, reciprocal, deep love happiness with your partner. **Love is an action verb**. We become better people in a positive long-lasting love relationship.

This dependence on another human being makes us stronger and able to better contribute to the world. This book ultimately aims not only to make you love happy, but also **for you to become a better person, and contribute to a better world**. I have a solid belief in the basic goodness and generosity of human nature.

I'm not dumb enough not to know that there are exceptions to goodness. You too try to find a virtuous person for yourself, and be brave enough to stay away from those who do not deserve you, who reject you. Our bond with another person is the #1 key to not only surviving, but to actually being in love happiness, thriving. **We are never so alive as when we are in love**.

Most of us, at the end of lives, will measure our life success by love: how deep we have loved; how sincerely we have been loved back. These were the best words of wisdom my mother passed on to me, and studies agree with her.

I have used 'he' or 'she' or 'they' in the book interchangeably, on purpose, to be gender neutral as much as possible. I have not used the word 'marriage' much, unless related to particular studies of married couples, because love happiness is much more than a legal contract. It's important towards the beginning of this book to clarify that **this is not a book about legal marriage**. A ceremony like a wedding or an official paper such as a marriage license does not usually make the love relationship more or less successful. We are going to stay well above all

4

this. Love instead should sustain itself over the years from the values and behaviors we will review in this book (for a sneak peak, see Tables 1-13 at the end of the book).

I also need to clarify that this is a book inclusive of **homosexual and heterosexual relationships, as well as transsexuals** (like my wonderful nephew), or any other LGBTQIA+ (lesbian, gay, bisexual, transgender, queer, questioning, intersex, asexual) person. The love we will discuss in these pages is blind to gender identities, cultures, religions, political creeds.

Love can happen and does happen to any of us, to any of you. It's wonderful to know that love is above the law, above gender identities, above religions, above cultures. It's so refreshing to think this way, as **'striving to help your partner to be happy' is universal**.

A romantic and sexual long-term committed relationship with another human being remains **the greatest gift life can offer**. Finally, I must admit I wrote this book **first and foremost for me**. I want love, I need love, I can't live without love. Now I am much clearer on the keys to achieve love happiness. It do hope the guidance in this book helps you out, too.

Definition of love

Unless you love someone, nothing else makes sense.
EE Cummings

Love is striving to help the other be happy. To me this is the best definition. It is a selfless, and also selfish wish. We need the person we love to be happy, for us to be happy ourselves. Love is altruistic. We should love in this manner our mother, our father, our kids, our relatives, our friends, our colleagues at work, all others really. **Romantic love** is this unselfish love aimed at our partner. In romantic love, we must do everything in our powers to make our partner happy.

The love partner can be a boy, a girl, a gay person like my wife's cousin, or a transsexual like my nephew; anyone really. One of the aims of romantic love should be to last for a long time. This book will show you the scientific tips to find true romantic love happiness, and make it last as long as possible. **The good news is, it mostly depends on you**.

We must spend time with our loved one, and allow her to spend time with family and friends. We must let her do what she likes to do most, be it surgery, hanging-out, debating, playing piano, dancing, or playing chess. We must try to let her pursuit her goals, so to achieve **meaningful (to her)** targets by using her best talents and strengths and eventually receiving a pat in the back, or whatever recognition she yearns for the most.

So love is not keeping her at home if she likes to socialize. Love is not inviting her to dance if she does not want to dance. Love is not bringing her into a crowd if she is shy. Love is not pushing her to run while she'd much rather walk. Love is not squashing her professional or personal calling, be it decreasing world's hunger or finding fossils in the desert.

Love is a bit hard too. Love means often to listen more than to talk. **Love is really, importantly, understanding the other.** Her dreams. Her likings. Love means not forcing your wishes on the other. Love means being flexible, and open.

6

And **love means, initially, knowing yourself well, so you can understand what person best matches you as a lover.** If you 'fall in love' with someone who always wants to ski, and you hate skiing, and you think you'll never like skiing, that relationship is not impossible, but certainly may not be the 'easy' love most of us yearn for.

Passionate vs empathic love

One is never in love with someone. One is just in love with the idea that one has built around another person, an idea previously developed and based on hope.

Anthony De Mello

The great thing is when you look in her eyes,
and she is looking back at you,
everything feels not quite normal,
because you feel stronger and weaker at the same time,
you feel excited and at the same time terrified.
The truth is you do not know what you feel,
but you know what kind of man you want to be.
It's as if you have reached the unreachable,
and you were not ready for it.

Spider Man

Passionate Love

Life is worth living because, once in a while, thank God, we fall in love with someone...

The scientific evidence has shown that the initial phase of love, what many call '**Falling in love,**' **lasts about 6 to 18 months**, for most people.[2] This phase has also been called Stage One of Love, or **Passionate Love**, or Obsessive Stage of Love, or the Spellbound phase.[3,4] I would call it, unfortunately, Short Term Love, too.

The Ancient Greeks described this love as '**eros,**' a life energy. This unstoppable urge drives us to **make a union, physical and emotional**, with a gratifying other being. **Passion** is best defined as a combination of sexual connection and attachment longing.

Love at this stage makes us feel we have found 'the one.' Our physical and emotional life is enhanced. We feel sensations which have our brain like on psychedelics. We **long to spend every second with our partner**. She is perfect. She has no flaws. The physical attraction is hardly containable. Our happiness depends on her every text, gaze, touch, word.

Before I ever knew this scientific fact, **as a teenager and then as a young adult in my twenties, I used to have this crazy personal rule.**[5] If by the end of the second year of a love relationship I was not feeling like ready to marry – i.e. to spend the rest of my life – with my girlfriend at the time, I would think about ending the relationship. I felt it would be honest to my partner to admit the 'flame' of love had dwindled.

My personal experience is that passionate love **can fire off from different sparks**. I remember falling for wonderful facial looks. For long thin legs. For height. For light eyes, or dark bright ones. But thankfully when I 'fell' for my wife it was for the way she was looking at me. That revealed her soul, her values, her belief in love. **Try to fall in love for character, values, not for looks**.

During passionate love, we truly **believe our partner is perfect**. He has no flaws. All we had hoped for in a partner, this new person seems to have. Since we do not know him well, we can project on him all our wishes, and easily pretend this person must have all the many qualities we have been looking for.

The initial spark is overwhelming. Just the appearance of a smile, before we have ever met and talked with the new person, opens the immediate mind leap that that person for sure is the answer to all of our wishes. Our brain suddenly imagines as if it was true that we are about to meet what will be our new sun, for the rest of our lives. There is **nothing reasonable about this phenomenon, it's all idealistic**. The longing is powerful, instantaneous, to us truer than truth.

Perhaps **our friends can see some flaws in our new lover, but we cannot**. Perhaps our new partner tells us even on the first date some of his major flaws, but we brush them aside. I made such assumptions so many times. I went out with a beautiful person and got engaged even if she told me within 30 minutes of our first meeting that she had tried suicide when her last boyfriend left her, and only emergency measures saved her. That did not phase me one bit; in fact I was happy to have the challenge to

9

make her happy - but it is really hard to make people happy when they are avoidant and depressed.

In this phase, we are **sure that we'll be forever happy** with this new partner. We cannot imagine living without him. Nothing else in life matters. Nobody else is even close to be as good a partner as this new person. **Love in this phase is easy**. It just happens. There is no work involved. You are floating through air, weightless.

You dream about the person. You wake up thinking about him. All day long, you think about what he is up to. He is in your last thoughts before you fall asleep. You cannot wait to get together again. And **you are sure he is going to have all the qualities you have been looking for**. He is going to check all the checks.

Every time you are together, things are just perfect. You can see only goodness, virtues, merits. We are blind to any defects, flaws, imperfections. **Passionate love is blind**, indeed. We just want to tell the other person, "I love you" so badly. Since the first moment. We think we have discovered the most precious thing.

If we find the courage to profess love, and get reciprocated – or if we are lucky to receive first the "I love you," and courageous enough to answer "I love you too," we just cannot wait to start to live the rest of our lives together, forever and ever.

Try to capture the splendid, unforgettable moment when a meeting, an initial early friendship, opens up on both sides to a more physical feeling, a wish to touch each other. Try to capture those seconds of opportunity. Take his hand and look in his eyes, give it a chance, open yourself up to a love prospect. Feel the butterflies. The tingles.

This is a time expert call '**of grace.**' We dive in a **state of grandiosity, of ecstasy**. Our brain is singing, carefree, gleeful, grateful of a gift we were not even imagining could be this wonderful. **Time ceases to exist**. Moments become eternal, unforgettable. We can now bear any difficulty. Our only focus is our partner, who gives us happiness just by being. Our imagination does the rest.

With our partner, when we fall in love, **time stops**. We are in '**flow.**' Flow is when we get into a mental state in which a person is completely focused on a single task or activity. We are directing all of our attention

10

towards the task, and we do not experience any thoughts about ourselves or what's going on around us, or about what time it is. We are oblivious to anything other than our partner. We are 'in the zone.' And this flow state, with time at a standstill, is happiness.

Don't be afraid to **join the revolution that passionate love brings**. Everything else now looks different. You see your parents, your siblings, your friends, in a different light. You start to explore changing home, changing city, changing job, changing group of friends. Passionate love brings with it a movement for a new life project. It creates new horizons, new opportunities, truly **an upheaval of the status quo** you had been living.

Something completely new is born when passionate love starts. Two individuals of different backgrounds, culture, looks, and DNA get connected by the sparkle of new love. Passionate love cancels initially these differences. Passionate love unites what was separated. The reaction towards revolution is not even seen as such by the new lovers. It's **uncontrollable. Irrepressible. Uncontainable. Overpowering.**

This is the time of writing poetry. Of obsessive texting at all hours of day and night. Of singing privately and publicly, even if we are tone deaf. **We go from hell, or at least the daily boring purgatory, to heaven. We reach paradise on earth.** We enter together with our partner the Garden of Eden.

This is also the time when **nothing becomes impossible**. We can travel across the country every weekend. We take off in winter storms. We spend much of the money we have. We have new strengths to do anything possible to allow the most time together. To achieve the most happiness with our lover.

We can forgo **eating, sleeping**, a comfortable dwelling. We can stand the most strenuous of circumstances. As long as we are together.

Falling in love brings a complete and radical **restructuring of our social world**. We might try to resist it at first, but if our mind keeps on going back to the new potential partner, we give in to the possibility of a new better life. It is like we are born again to a **new life**. Our being gets renewed.

As we fall in love, we see even the world, not only other beings, in a new light. We are changing, and so our eyes see everything else around us as mutated. **Nature is kinder, more florid**. The weather is beautiful even when raining. Snowing is a chance for snow angels. The world in general is now stunning, because our lover is in it.

Hopefully our new partner and the elation of new love brings with it a **new you, a better you, a you closer to the you that you were always supposed to be**. You get closer to being the true you. A true you that you might not even have known was possible.

We love to make the other happy; but even more **we love because we always needed to; we were just waiting for the right partner. We love first and foremost to make ourselves happy**. We love the other 'selfishly,' as her happiness from our love makes us happy.

Another perk of passionate love is that **we feel validated**. We more than anyone else are aware of our weaknesses, and shortcomings. Now we find someone who seems to love us nonetheless. Feeling loved back means **we are worth. We suddenly have value**.

We always knew inside ourselves that we had inherent value. We appreciate ourselves in some ways, we are aware we have some character traits that are desirable. Now **through seeing someone else, a prior stranger, fall in love with us, our whole persona gets validated**. We get recognized as worthy of marvelous love.

After childhood, parental love is not enough anymore. We know our mother loves us no matter what. Mom and dad are not objective. But this new person must be objective; **her love means I'm worth it! She does recognize my uniqueness, and loves it**. Love is a powerful confidence booster. It demonstrates tangibly we are admirable, valuable.

Finally we feel we are meeting what we were born for. Finally there is a person who understands us. Finally there is a person who appreciates us even knowing our innermost feelings. Finally **the destiny we were afraid to dream of, becomes reality**.

The past gets seen in a new light. In fact the past gets seen as almost irrelevant compared to the new present joy. The past is prehistory. The real history of our life starts with our new passionate love. We form a new community with our partner. And the past almost disappears. We forget a bit family and friends. We are completely captured by the hope of a new future, radically different from what was yesterday. We also **absolve our new lover from any bad past.**

Falling in love means also **finding extreme interest in the other person**. We want long answers describing her family, her upbringing, her life experiences. We love every story. We can't get enough narrations about her.

Falling in love usually involves also **tangible small gifts of belonging**. A bracelet. Earrings. A new wallet. A cheap ring. A necklace. Some sign that that person is ours now. Some sign from our lover that makes us feel like we are with him all day and night. And that he is not afraid to display to the world our new commitment.

Life can be full of dullness. The routine of job, house chores, social duties other organize but we do not enjoy. We are dragging along. Waking up to another Ground Hog Day, dull of the same monotony. **Falling in love introduces a blinding light into our daily routine opacity.**

The more barriers there are, the stronger is passionate love. Obstacles make passionate love more desirable at times, more longed for. Falling in love wants to build something new, and therefore **needs to destroy something old.** You feel now **torn between the love for your parents, original family, and the need to spend instead >90% of your time and efforts in your new community**: you and your partner.

The history of the world is the history of love. **Love is a revolution which brings cataclysm change in our own world, but also the world at large**. Our choice to fall in love brings major consequences to our family, our friends, our job, our 'village.' Changes in the village have an effect through the world at large.

It's important to **avoid blood baths in this battle**. Parents, friends, community, village, all need to understand we as human beings are evolving in a better person by falling in love. Parents in particular – how hard for me to rationalize! – need to accept this is a natural evolution through revolution.

As parents, we need to realize that it's not that the being - our child - does not love us anymore. But our daughter has evolved to a being capable of falling in love with a stranger, and so moves closer to

13

happiness. And if we want her happiness, we need to let her go towards what she longs for.

Don't be afraid of being rejected. It is much worse years later to remember a missed chance at love, than to remember you at least gave it a try, and someone else missed out, not you. **Love's worst enemy is inaction**. Like happiness, love is continuous motion, forward motion, taking chances, being reborn, even with the same partner.

Love requires trust in our partner, transparency, letting go of barriers, being truthful to our overwhelming feelings. Love requires the courage to believe in others. Love requires the other to believe we are unique, special, extraordinary, just like we think our new partner is unique, special, extraordinary.

We need to feel indispensable to the happiness of our partner, like our partner is indispensable to our happiness. We abandon ourselves to another human being, trusting he will take good care of us. Love is hope in positivity and altruism.

The other person is indeed unique. She has a mix of qualities nobody else has. Those special traits are present only in her, nobody else. **Thinking our partner is uniquely fit to make us love happy is a sign of true deep love**. Being loved back by this person makes us feel a better being. Gives us strength. Makes us proud. **We walk above the clouds**, with our chin up, with new confidence in ourselves.

Some places, like the one where we met, or where we exchanged our first kiss, **become sacred**. A street. A city. A piece of grass. They become immortal in our existence. Love brings with it a new religion full of holy moments, objects, spaces.

Passionate love is **the love we see in commercials**, read in romance books, watch in romantic comedies. It's the love that occurs at the beginning of a relationship. Those are the first few weeks, at times few blissful months, of 'blind love.'

The partner, who we do not know well yet, has no fault. We project on her our dreams, identikit, hopes. We imagine her being exactly what we are looking for. **Everything she does is magic, really**.

We believe that **our partner is omnipotent**. That our partner can guess our needs, and fulfill them. The partner has all we need, and he can

14

and will give it to us, as we always dreamed it would happen in a perfect world.

We believe our partner to be **omnipresent**. We believe our partner is always available to meet our needs. And that they have no major needs of their own.

In Japanese Buddhism, there are two forms of happy life: *nin* and *ten*. *Nin* is the world of peace and daily tranquility. *Ten* is the extraordinary moment of emotion. A day of *nin* equals to a year of happy tranquility. But **a day of *ten* corresponds to one thousand elated, blissful years**. The elation of love after its initial spark makes us feel, in that moment, eternal, as if in paradise: we are in *ten*. **The feelings of those initial magical moments stay in our memories forever**.

Emotion is the great motivator. Emotion comes from the Latin 'e' and 'movere,' meaning 'to move out.' Emotion moves us to do something. Emotion transforms an object into a memento. Emotion transforms a person into the love of our lives. It makes us more vulnerable, but also better known to the world.

Passionate love involves four phenomena, as described by Dr Hendrix.[6] The first is the phenomenon of **recognition**, when we say something like, "I know we have just met, but I somehow feel like I already know you." The second is the phenomenon of **timelessness**, as we say, "It seems like we have always been together; I do not remember when I did not know you."

The third is the phenomenon of **reunification**, as we say, "When I'm with you, I no longer feel alone. I feel finally whole, complete." And the fourth phenomenon is that of **necessity**, when we say, "I love you so much, I cannot live without you."

Often passionate love starts with infatuation. We can fall for looks. For irresistible sexual attraction. Or money. Or fame. Or fear of losing something. Or for competitiveness. Or for wanting to dominate someone. Or to be dominated.

During this full attraction phase, the brain releases a lot of **dopamine and norepinephrine**. Production of endorphins and enkephalins is also increased by the brain, as well the neurotransmitter serotonin. These chemicals make us feel like on a 'high,' like on drugs, now immersed in a dreamy reality. The right hemisphere of our brain is the emotional part. It is particularly responsive, for example, to verbal clues, such as facial expression and tone of voice.

It is **often in this obsessed stage of love that many start living together, or get married. Long-term commitments such as marriage should not be made in this early passionate phase**, when really you do not know the partner enough. Parents and grandparents have been saying this for generations, but we still do not believe them when we are so dazzled, blinded, by the hormonal and psychological revolution of passionate love.

There are a few **good comparisons to understand the difference between passionate, short-term love, and empathic, long-term love**. At the beginning, in passionate love, we are like a **near-sighted person without glasses**. The passion does not make us see any faults in the other. The blur makes everything perfect; makes everything like we would imagine it in a perfect partner.

At some point, sooner or later, though, we do get the glasses back on our face. And then we can see well, and see the partner in all his glory as well as his non-virtues. Hopefully in our regained 20/20 vision we still like what we have as a partner.

Passionate love can be compared to taking off, lifting off ground like when flying, and reaching above the clouds, in an heavenly state. **Empathic love is the eventual safe landing on solid ground**, a state of being that can last forever, even if not as glamorous as taking off for a new adventure and seeing the sun above the clouds.

Empathic love has the benefit of having both feet on the ground. But it should strive to often try to take off and reach the sun with moments of intimacy, trips, events together, etc. **Passionate love is something ideal; emphatic love is something real**.

Aristotle described three kinds of love relationships, making a similarity also between love and friendship. Love can be useful, pleasurable or good. Passionate love is the stage when love is useful, and pleasurable. Empathic love instead is love that is good, i.e. the person focuses on the other and love comes from wanting the best for the other, as a giver, and not as a taker because of what use or pleasure she gets in return.

Aristotle actually concluded that if friendship, and love, become good, the usefulness and the pleasure follow anyway. While if we put usefulness or pleasure as ultimate goals, friendship and love do not last, and do not become good.

Another similar image can be drawn between passionate/empathic love and flower/fruit. The flower - passionate love - is the initial beauty, the colors of irresistible attraction, the superb display of our better traits. The flower eventually gives rise to the fruit – empathic love, which can sustain us for much longer.

Both the flower and the fruit are beautiful. But different. We just need to learn to appreciate the difference, and not confound them. Flowers are transitory. Fruits can be stored much longer. Solid ground is forever; being over the clouds can only last so long.

As adults, it's important to realize that **the unique emotions of the first time you locked eyes, the first date, the first kiss, the first time you made love, the first vacation, are just that, unique**. They do not happen again. To expect the same butterflies for 50 years is childish. It is so unfortunate that the movies and social media end always at the time a couple finally gets together, and seldom cover what follows passionate love.

After all these years, now I know I was feeling what most scientists have said is a natural evolution, the end of **'passionate' love**, when as an adolescent and in my twenties I would feel the butterflies disappear after about a year and a half in a love relationship.

The more important part of love is what happens after the initial phase of passionate love. **What does it take to be happy with the same romantic partner for a long-time, hopefully for a lifetime? This is what we want to know, and this is what I'm hoping to concentrate in. It is reckless to go through life without knowing the principles for long-term empathic love.**

Empathic love

Empathic love is less selfish than passionate love. Empathic love is also called Stage Two of Love, Compassionate love, Covenant Stage of love,[3] Real Love,[7] Mature Love, or Long-Term Love. I love to call it empathic because empathy is the ability to understand and share the feelings of another human being.

Empathy involves altruism, wanting to make the other person happier, healthier. Compassionate as a word is too religious, pious. With passionate love, we look out for ourselves, we try to get from our partner things that pleasure us. Passionate love is selfish. Empathic love is altruistic.

The Ancient Greeks described this love as **'agape.'** Agape is the self-transcending love that redirects 'eros,' the life force, away from oneself and instead towards one's partner. Agape is unconditional **altruistic love** for another person.

Part of this ultimate stage of love is also **'philia,'** another Greek word which means **'love between friends.'** It's key to communicate well as a friend with our partner. It's important that love happens between equals, just as friends should be.

There are **two principal components** of empathic love. **First, the will to love. Second, knowledge of the nature of love - striving to help the other be happy the way he wants to be happy.** Love is not the illusion of our dreams projected into the partner as in passionate love. Empathic love entails us knowing ourselves well, our partner well, and accepting her as we accept ourselves, unconditionally.

Empathic love is a **choice.** The spontaneous, impulsive and unplanned euphoria of passionate love turns into a conscious, rational will to be with someone long-term, in good as well as bad times. Enthusiasm changes with time into loving dedication towards the human being we chose as a partner.

We finally understand than an **even higher form of love happiness** is to **make our partner happy the way she wants to be loved**. After many years, with empathic love, we have hopefully gotten to know well our partner. Empathic love is not the buying act that is passionate love.

Empathic love is us giving our best effort to make our partner happy. **It's in giving, rather than receiving**, that we truly touch the **pinnacle of love happiness**. Think Mother Theresa, Jesus, saints, volunteers everywhere, or whomever other altruist you admire. True greatness is expressed in serving.

We finally realize that our behavior affects the other's happiness. We study how our partner likes to be loved. We **learn about their preferences, their attachment styles, their love languages**, what they like for us to do for them.

So we consciously make the choice to **learn to express love in the other person's love language**. If the other person likes to spend time one-on-one for over an hour every day, we plan for that. If she likes compliments, or gifts, we purposely give them out to her.

The desire to please our partner makes us change ourselves some. We do have certain traits we like to be loved for; but sometimes our partner appreciate other deeds that might not come so naturally at first. Love pushes us to modify a bit who we are, to appease our lover, to make her happy. Love revolutionizes who we are, not only others and the world around us.

The path to empathic love includes those days in which we realize, after the blinding of passionate love, that our partner sees the world at times differently than us. That he likes vanilla more than chocolate, unlike us. That sports, our passion, is not much his thing.

Empathic love is not blind anymore, and becomes aware of the inescapable differences between two beings. In a way, we should be called *Homo empathicus* to be able to excel at long-term love.

Empathic love has **a window open on the inner soul of the other**. And sees inside the good, the similar, the bad, the different. And still decides to continue the love commitment. Empathic love does not need to day dream, as passionate love does. Empathic love rationally decides to **forgive** what we don't like as much in our partner.

In empathic love, we each know each others' weaknesses, but, even if we are aware they are indeed weaknesses, we understand them, we embrace them, in fact in the end she appreciates his weaknesses. Perhaps these weaknesses are expressions of altruism, of generosity, of enthusiasm. There is beauty in these partner's weaknesses.

The partner who loves empathically can now only see himself as reaching towards the truth when confronting his views with her views. He appreciates the differences, and the dissimilar points of view. She thinks that the truth is better reached as we look at the sphere from differing angles.

This way, **each lover feels her unique prospective is validated**, heard, even if not always agreed on. Each partner sees the same value in the other's opinion. This much wider prospective enriches reality, makes it clearer.

Empathic love **must be fed and nurtured.** It does not always come easy, but requires continuous focus on making our partner happy. **The illusion of having a flawless partner which occurred during passionate love, disappears**, and we do see the limitations and even failures of our loved one. We need to begin to love those imperfections too.

Empathic love is **mature love**. Empathic love is wisdom that we too are imperfect, and so we cannot pretend perfection. It's the deep understanding that our partner has so many great qualities, those most important to us. And that those virtues vastly win over the imperfections.

Empathic love must evolve and surpass in some way from what we used to consider as romantic – wordless intuitions, instantaneous longings, a blind mindless image of our partner. These stand in the way of learning how to really be with someone long-term. Love eventually becomes a skill, with mature enthusiasm rather than mindless enthusiasm.

Nobody has ever had perfect love. Once we comprehend this, we can have a shot at trying to achieve empathic love. **This is impossible if we believe the fairytale of "And they lived happily thereafter."** Do not believe this myth. Long-term love requires commitment and hard work.

Empathic love is a commitment to **love no matter what the difficulties**. It is intentional love. It is conscious love – not unconscious stuporous love as in passionate love. It's love with open eyes, aware of the bright sides as well as the darker sides. It requires thought and action.

Empathic, long-term love should also rely on the relationship attitude we had when we were young. Empathic love can only continue if we focus less on our past broken-heart love relationships, and more on the **positive attitude** we started with, and the positives we saw in others and in our own relationships. Empathic love truly **comes from an open heart still believing in love**, despite the occasional hurts along life.

Interesting, **during passionate love we long for qualities of empathic love**. During passionate love, we hope for eventual stability, a home, daily routines. During empathic love instead, when a home and routines are established, we long for the past times of desire, ecstasy, extraordinary events.

Time can be a great help in consolidating empathic love. Moments of happiness lived together accumulate, and form an ever deeper bond. **Gratitude** as well accumulates over time, as we should recollect all the moments when our partner has been there for us, in good as well as in trying time.

Eventually **empathic love forms two different individuals, who are at the same time a unity**. They are fused in some ways. Family, friends, society, all can see and can feel a link bonding the two partners in empathic love, as they are independent but also stronger as they are a couple; they can rely on each other. People can count on the fact that one empathic lover will support and be strongly bound to her partner, and vice versa.

Empathic love also brings some organization after the revolution. Parents, initially ignored, need to be brought into the knowledge of the new structure. **Say two divorcees are now a couple.** Their respective kids might have been a bit surprised by the new partnership. They need to be included in the new family. They need to feel loved and included by their parent.

Mature empathic love often gets to be proven in its longevity after the couple becomes empty-nesters. As the kids leave the house, two individuals who went through initial passionate love, formed a strong bod capable of producing and raising kids, now find themselves alone, one on one. At this point if empathy for each other is still there, empathic mature love happiness can be enjoyed for the rest of their lives. If the

21

connection had become parenting and not much more, the disconnection becomes overt and inescapable.

Passionate love can only develop into long-term love if it is balanced love. In the beginning, passionate love is usually started by one partner. The one who falls in love. Occasionally both partners feel the sparkle, fall equally head over heels for each other. But most often only one person gets the tingles, makes the first move, declares her feelings.

In this common situation, a possible first scenario is that the **receiving person is just not interested**, and the love relationship never starts. But there are **two other possible scenarios**. One is that **the other person soon sees the sparkle as well, gets the tingles, and falls in love** as well. This other person must have been already also predisposed to love, open to love. This means that **it is possible to make someone fall in love with us**. But he needs to be ready and willing. Timing is everything. An open heart is a must.

In the third scenario, **the other person feels interested, flattered, but does not fall in love.** He is open to love, just not sure this is the right person, but worth a try for a bit. This person lives love as a reflection of the 'fallen-in-love' partner.

In these **unbalanced** relationships, one person feels she cannot live without her partner; the other partner is not as committed, is not lost in ecstasy, has his eyes wide open, no butterflies in his stomach. Only rationality – "She is nice enough, and treats me great" – keeps him in the relationship.

The rational lover sees problems as problems of the partner, not like his own; 'couple problems' are not shared by the person not in love. The rational person does not see any problems. The true lover is indeed alone; **fire burns only on her side.** The true lover begins to imagine a world that does not exist, in which she is loved.

The **not-in-love** partner accuses the other of living in Lalaland. The in-love one continues to ask, "Do you love me?" And desperately continues to shower the other with acts of kindness, gifts, gentle hugs, compliments. Asking for continuous proofs of love, for any hint of being reciprocated.

But **love can't be bought** in these situations. One cannot make another fall in love if they do not want to. It's sad to see that some of these couples even get married. And some even 'survive' together for a lifetime. With neither partner ever being truly happy. **Who wants to love without being reciprocated?**

It is hard to break these relationships, because the in-love person wants to imagine any clue of being loved back. The more one waits to break such a relationship, the more pain she will suffer. Realizing in the end that, "He never loved me;" "I wasted so much time an effort."

On the other side, **the not-in-love one is content to just have a person physically next to them.** Perhaps for economic reasons. Perhaps for security at night. Perhaps because his parents want him married. Or because society sees married couple as positive examples. He does not care much about the other person being miserable.

He cares about the institution of being materially together, not the deep romantic intimacy of love. He despises falling in love as irrational, despicable, weak. These partners live on different planets, both in cold places, light years away from each other.

Some of us see **love as a refuge**, and the partnership of two becomes all we want. Some of us instead take love as the biggest part of our well-being, but **aim to integrate it with the larger garden of other family** members, and friends. Studies seems to show that the latter may be associated with more happiness, but it all depends on the couple specific preferences.

Empathic love is also the time when the strong bond can allow a **healthy introduction of kids**. A baby shifts again the balance of relationships. For the mother in particular, this is a new falling in love. Before the Oedipal complex, where the baby is in love with his mother, the Laio complex sees the father being envious of the maternal love towards her son.

Mom, dad, and the new baby person should embrace the new structure, and buy into the fact that our hearts are big enough for all these loves, and these relationships. In fact the gratitude for a daughter or son should vastly overwhelm any hints towards the Laio complex.

About 67% of couples experience a drop in marital satisfaction in the three years after the birth of their first baby. Some studies also report that kids per se do not enhance parental happiness – even I see it differently based on my own experience. Be careful, **do not forget to love your partner after a baby arrives**.

Empathic love in a couple is put to the test again when the kids leave the house, for a job, a mate, and/or college. Sue Johnson, the author of Love Sense, calls this phase Mature Love.[3] It is the ultimate test to see if the partners really want to stay together, not just to rear kids, but to pleasure each other, particularly emotionally, for the rest of their lives.

Psychiatrists says that many people in their 50's experience a new kind of adolescence. Suddenly, like an adolescent, they have major life choices to make again. While during parenthood they had more tasks and less personal freedom, their kids leaving the nest means parents have free evenings, weekends, often some money and time to spare. Doing what??

Is staying with the parent of our kids the best choice? Is he making you happy, love happy? Or, once the kids' love and emotional support is cut off, do we need to seek love happiness elsewhere, as we are unable to feel it from our current partner? In many studies, the peak incidence of divorce is after around 18-22 years of marriage, e.g. after the kids leave the home.

Benefits of love

Nobody has his head completely on his shoulders.
Find the woman who will put your head square on your shoulders.

In the mind:
  most important – happiness
  most insignificant – insecurity
  most brutal – loneliness
  most wonderful – love.
                    Anna Berghella

I love you not for who you are, but for who I am when I'm with you.
                    Gabriel García Márquez

The benefits of emphatic long-term love are innumerous (Table 2).[8] They include better health, higher levels of happiness, happier kids and people around you, and even a better financial situation. These facts derive from multiples scientific studies comparing people in happy long-term relationships, compared to single people and people in unhappy relationships. Many studies compare married to unmarried persons.

In terms of *health*, partners in happy long-term relationships enjoy much better health. Emotional support and other benefits of empathic love **lower blood pressure; decrease cardiac disease; decrease chance of dying of heart problems**. A study showed that married couples who have coronary bypass surgery are three times more likely to be alive 15 years later than their unmarried counterparts.

The **immune system** of happy married couples or couples in positive relationships is stronger than single adults, and helps **prevent infections**. Happy relationships **decrease your chances of getting sick by 35%**. Happy couples also have **less arthritis**. More pain tolerance.[9]

These partners enjoy both a **lower chance of getting cancer** (e.g. a 30% lower chance of prostate cancer), and a **reduced death rate from cancer**.

They have **less stress; less anxiety; less depression**. They are more resilient against stress and trauma. A study showed that eighteen months after a tragedy, married persons have fewer signs of post-traumatic stress disorder, and less depression.

They therefore benefit from **less substance abuse, psychosis, violence, and suicide**.

Long-term love is associated with **better concentration, a more positive outlook, increased mental health**.

Long-term happy love is ultimately associated with a **longer life**. This blissful condition can extend your life by 4-8 years compared to partners of unhappy relationships.

In terms of *mood*, persons in happy long-term empathic relationships with positive-attitude partners are **happier**; they have happier kids; they have **more sex** than single friends. A study reported that husbands in particular who are helpful at home get more sex in the relationship.

In term of *financials*, happy-in-long-term-love people are better off financially, and, if married, pay less taxes and enjoy hundreds of federal perks. The higher financial wealth can decrease anxiety and stress, and these partners are therefore more optimistic.

The mental benefits of happy relationships are a **virtuous cycle**, which starts early in life. Studies have shown that the more you smile in childhood photos, the less you get divorced. Divorce is also contagious: your chance of getting divorced is 75% higher if your friends get divorced.

The **benefits of a happy couple expand even outside the two partners** directly involved. We become **better parents**. And the magic circle continues. The best thing you can do for your child is to create a loving environment, where she feels unconditionally loved, as you felt you received from your parent.

This waterfall effect will transmit probably **not just to your kids, but also to their partners, and then to their kids**. It's the example that matters, more than what you say, as everything else in education.

These are **societal benefits** of long-term love between two individuals. Adults who feel loved by their partner are **more empathic to others**. These love partners have **more energy** for themselves, and to give

26

to others. They **see others more positively**. They are **more willing to engage with others**. Feeling loved makes people **kinder and more tolerant**.

The ironic paradox is that being dependent on somebody's love makes us more **independent**. The pyramid of life (Figure 1) has at its base Security. If our emotional state is **secure**, if we feel we are loved and supported by our partner (as we were originally by our mother/father/parents/caregiver), then **we can take on the world**. We are **free of the worry of our own safety**.

Love happiness is a building block to **achieve our self-actualization** (Figure 1). Securely attached people show **fewer discrepancies between their stated ideal and actual traits**. People in love happiness are more **attuned to others' emotions**, and are therefore **much better leaders**.

We humans have survived and thrive as a species by letting our emotions link to others, through caring and cooperating. Sue Johnson, one of the foremost experts in love, calls us *Homo vinculum*, "one who bonds."

A positive love relationships brings **joy and contentment, safety and trust, intense interest and involvement, curiosity and openness**. Positive relationships make us **more resilient, advance our personal growth**. They make us more apt to be **community builders, creative workers, good leaders, and caring citizens**.

Better relationships between love partners are indeed a **social good**. They create a wave of warmth, of love, of caring, of altruism. They can create a kinder world. We all need one another, more than ever in this globally connected world. We are truly mutually dependent.

Being in love makes you, in brief, a healthier, better, and better-off person. **Why all these benefits?** Much is from the consistent emotional support of the love partner. **Spouses keep after each other to eat healthy, to exercise, to have regular medical check-ups, to take medicine.** But perhaps the best health benefit is that happy couples **spend time to listen to each other and keep their relationship positive**, which has all the health benefits.

A **hormone linked with 'love' is oxytocin**. It's the 'medication' I've probably prescribed the most in my professional life as an obstetrician. It was discovered in 1909, and its benefits keep on being revealed. It's both a neurotransmitter and a hormone. As a neurotransmitter, it communicates with the brain and nervous system. As a hormone, it communicates with organ systems, too, as the breast and genitals.

Oxytocin is naturally released during breastfeeding to help produce more milk. But also during orgasm. Some call oxytocin the 'cuddle' hormone, the 'love' hormone. Studies have shown that **just thinking about our loved one triggers release of oxytocin** in our body.[3] Physiologically, oxytocin makes us more biologically driven to be associative, altruistic, responsive to other's (in this case our partner's) needs.

Another benefit of oxytocin is that it turns off our threat detector, the amygdala, as well as the hypothalamic-pituitary-adrenal (HPA) axis. This HPA system is the 'get ready for challenge or threat' part of our nervous system. And oxytocin also turns on the parasympathetic system, i.e. the calming, 'relax-all-is-fine' part of our nervous system.

I'm not sure anyone has devised it, but a 'minute-by-minute' oxytocin level detector could be used to measure how relaxed, cuddly, 'in love' we are when we are with our loved one.

It's a catch-22 virtuous circle. Oxytocin generates a sense of trust and calm, trust generates closeness and sex, orgasm stimulates oxytocin, and around it goes again (Figure 2). Isn't it great? We just have to start the circle somewhere.

Other areas of the brain have lots of oxytocin receptors. For example, the region of the brain that is key to retrieving memories, the **hippocampus**, enables us to better put together old love images and memories giving us chemical boosts during romantic moments.

Oxytocin receptors are also plentiful in the **nucleus accumbens**, the area of the brain that is central to the production of dopamine, which is the neurotransmitter that makes us feel elated and euphoric. Studies have shown that oxytocin increases release of dopamine, which helps then further support attachment between partners, as we perceive we are

28

having a really good time. We tend to stick around people who give us pleasure, who make us feel content.

Interestingly, women have more oxytocin, and less testosterone. Testosterone is associated instead with aggressiveness, with the will to conquer, to win, to be number one at the detriment of our partner. I wish we could magically increase oxytocin in the right places, and decrease testosterone in some key areas of the brain of us humans!

The message is clear: you have to work on your relationship every day (Tables 6,7,12,13), as this will do more for your health and longevity than working out at a health club (Table 2). For example, studies have shown that **twenty minutes of quality time a day between loving partners have 3 times the health benefits than the same time devoted to exercise.**

Nothing makes us healthier, stronger and happier than a loving, stable, long-term secure bond with another human being. Psychologist Bert Uchino of the University of Utah states that a good love relationship is the best recipe for good health, and the most powerful antidote to aging and death.

Attachment

The first and foremost instinct of humans is neither sex nor aggression. It is to seek contact and comforting connection.
Sue Johnson

Our brain thrives on **social connection** from the day we are born. Studies as well as my experience as a father - I have four children - show that **emotional affection is what babies want, since birth. Adult romantic love is similar to the attachment bond between mother, or father, and child**.

Our **innate need to depend on another human being** never goes away. When we call for help, we need to be able to count on someone who we know will be there for us. **It's as fundamental a need as needing water, food, shelter**. In fact, in many ways food and water are sustenance, and a good warm hug is 'life itself.' Love is not the icing on the cake of life; **love is a primary basic need, like oxygen**.

Drs. John Bowlby, a British psychiatrist, the father of the attachment theory, and Mary Ainsworth, have described **3 ways we interact with others** in relationships, first as children, then as adults: **secure; anxious; avoidant** (Table 3).

Interesting, these patterns were discovered **first in children** in the 1950's and 1960's. The studies observed children when the primary caregiver, usually the mother, leaves the room they are in. Secure children miss their mother, but continue to stay serene, smiling widely upon their mother's return in the room.

Anxious children start crying as the mother leaves the room, and stay quite agitated, up until the mother returns. They continue to attempt to get the mother to come back until she does. Even when the mother does return to their room, these children remain anxious, unsure how long the mother will stay.

Avoidant children do not flinch as the mother leaves the room. They stay content alone. They barely notice when the mother comes back. They have learned to live in solitude, and not to count on others for company or for help.

The fundamental simple discovery is that we as humans are born to need ongoing, nearby, reassuring physical and emotional connection with our parent(s). Often one in particular, usually our mother. Since the moment we are born, we need love just as much as water, food, oxygen, shelter.

Studies have shown that a good nurturing secure bond with a parent when we are one year old, predicts the ability to have positive close intimate secure love relationships with a partner when we get to adulthood.

Studies have also shown that **children finish developing their love attachment styles between 5 and 8 years old**. And these depend mostly on their parents' relationships, and in general on the love relationship they have been most exposed to. And **it depends first and foremost on how they were loved – or not – by their parent(s)**.

There are children who are **secure** in their pattern of attachment. They were loved by their parent(s), and they know that, when a parent gets out of their sight, they will come back. **They know that if they need help, the parent/caregiver will come to help them. They know they can count on that person**.

They can play alone for a while, as their love is reciprocated, and **when they need the help from their trusted other, they will get it**. In fact, having a secure figure allows these children to explore an unknown environment, to take risks, to develop, to learn, to be in serene flow.

A person develops a secure attachment style **when her parents are sensitive and responsive to her needs**. Such a child learns that she can rely on her parents, confident that they'll be available to her whenever she needs them. Children of mothers who were sensitive to their needs are more likely to have a secure attachment style, studies show.

Positive maternal conditions such as **marital satisfaction, low stress, no depression, and social support from extended family and friends**, all make it for a better mother and therefore a higher chance of a secure child. These mothers (and/or father or closest caregiver) possess a clear sense to detect when their child wants to be held. **They can sense their child emerging distress and act upon it before she turns into full-blown crying**.

I myself benefited from the secure love of my mother. She always loved me, and still does at 85 years old, **unconditionally**. I have been able to count on her secure love so much that I was able to do anything I wanted in life. Her secure bond was my launching pad in the world, being able to literally explore the planet and discover my passions, callings, and finding therefore my true self. Thanks to her, I was really never worried about my emotional safety.

Life is not just the survival of the fittest, in terms of the healthiest. It's really first and foremost **survival of the most nurtured**.[3] If our 100 billion neurons, especially those in the right brain, were exposed to parental love since day 1 of our life, we are going to be so much happier and successful in life.

The **ultimate in parenting, the pinnacle of being a good parent, is to deeply understand your child primary love languages, and love them the way they like to be loved**. And also teach them there are other love languages that might be very important to others.

Speaking all 5 love languages makes us not only better people, but in particular better partners, better friends, better colleagues at work, better siblings, better sons and daughters, etc.

Let's make an example: after a trip, you bring the same teddy bear as a gifts for your two kids. One jumps up from joy and starts playing with it – love language: gifts. The other is thankful, but quickly tosses the teddy bear aside, and asks about your trip – love language: quality time.

There is nothing wrong about any of your kids, they are both wonderful. You can support them so much as they grow up by helping them to discover who they are and what they like, and catering to their strengths and needs.

Observe also **how they love you. Listen to their requests. Listen to their complaints**. My two older sons are wonderful, and different. One likes acts of service, and quality time. The other likes physical touch, and words of affirmation. I must continue to remind myself this, and love them the way they like to be loved, without forcing my love languages onto them. I am not perfect, but I do try hard every day.

The child absorbs this idyllic situation of the secure bond with the parent. The child **becomes an adult capable of the same gift of being**

able to comfort, sooth, love, be supportive, be present. It becomes for them an innate talent made stronger by the 'village' she grew up with as a youngster.

The most valuable gift a parent can give her child – and a lover can give his lover – is emotionally attuned attention, and timely responsiveness. A study has shown that the strength of a bond between a one-year-old baby and her mother predicts how good the person became at dealing with their emotions and resolving conflicts at age twenty-one.[3]

Additionally, a **genetically easy temperament** is another factor which helps the child to become later a secure adult. A tranquil temperament makes it easier for parents to be loving and responsive to the child.

Other children are **anxious** in their relationship with their caregiver. The children who act anxious are those whose parents were not around, were perhaps drug addicts, or could not be present for whatever other reasons. The child learned since young that **there would be a caregiver around, but not always**.

In these early relationships, **sometimes their parent would come back to help them when needed, sometimes they would not.** This would cause these children to always be anxious. The going out of the room by a parent would cause them major anxiety, as they were not sure when, and perhaps if, the parent would return.

The third and last type of attachment in relationship – the **avoidant** one - develops in those children who were so **exposed to unsecure parent/caregiver relationship**, that they at some point **stopped worrying about being helped at all, as they mostly could not count on anyone** helping them.

They were so deeply hurt by the lack of trust and love by the parent, that they **stopped expecting anything**. These include also children who were abused, and avoid actual contact with others. They are afraid of others. Or these are even children who had a parent who ignored them, and clearly preferred another sibling.

Some of this goes back to the earliest experiences in our life. When we were in the womb everything – usually – was provided without us asking. As infants though, we needed someone to tend to us. In the crib, we had just one cry to ask for food, warmth, water, breastmilk, attention, a change of diaper.

If nobody came to rescue us as we were **crying desperately in the crib**, we became wary of others' help and input. We stopped trusting people who were not us. While if we did have at least one person who came quickly to help, we developed trust in other human beings. **Good feelings and bad feelings were created now by the action of other people**. Avoidants did not have someone who came to help them.

Separation distress in children, as in adults, begins as **first step with anger and protest**. The second step is **clinging and seeking**. The third step, if separation continues without reassurance, is marked by **depression and despair**. The final step is **detachment**. And nobody recovers from detachment. It becomes a part of someone's being, unfortunately. They will decline attachment to another human being for the rest of their lives.

These children were devastated by the lack of being loved, and so avoid love relationship. They do not trust others, sadly. They can only trust themselves; they therefore minimize closeness, avoiding being hurt again. They **cherish independence, and equate intimacy with a loss of their beloved independence**.

They scorn people who openly declare their 'counting' on others for support and for love. These children, even if well fed, failed to develop normally, given the lack of an attachment figure; they had stunted psychological growth, as well as intellectual, social and emotional problems. The emotional starvation has profound and usually ever-lasting effects.

The avoidant adult can only resolve some of these issues if he is able to open up and explore, deeply inside himself, where he learned to discount his needs for emotional connection. Where he felt so left alone that he gave up on the possibility of being intimate, connected, with anyone ever. And of course, the positive path forward includes being able to share the honest, profound personal answers with his partner.

I state often, half-jokingly, that **there is no parent who does not ruin their kids.** Our children copy everything from us. If you love the Yankees, they will probably love them too. We unfortunately also tell

34

them directly at times that they are not smart; that they cannot do math; that they are not coordinated; that their friend is smarter than them; that they cannot dance; and so on.

Our example, and these comments, hit deeply the children's souls. We unfortunately believe our parents, and are thwarted from growing to our full potential as our own parents did not gives us unconditional love, a positive example to follow, and did not believe in us.

If our mother or father tells us sex is bad, we will probably believe that. We believe them if they tell us as children that boys only want to touch us; or that true love does not exist; or that happiness is an impossible dream; or that life is hard and just a series of disappointments.

Some parents tell their child she is only good at something. They approved only part of us, not the full self. And the way our parents most influenced us was by example. If our parents were a bad example of a loving relationship, our chance for divorce and unhappy love life increases.

Unfortunately, we can only be as good as our parents raised us to be. That is why I often say one should first study, and get a diploma and **a license to be a parent** before being allowed to replicate oneself.

These early attachments styles, which usually continue in adult life, persisted over evolution as each can have some evolutionary advantage. The four basic elements of attachment involve: 1. Seeking out and maintaining emotional and physical connection with our loved one; 2. Reaching out to our loved one in particular in times of threat, or upset; 3. Missing them when they are physically or emotionally remote; and 4. Depending on them emotionally.

These attachment systems are the mechanisms in our brain responsible for tracking and monitoring the safety and availability of the persons we are attached to. As children, these people are usually our parents. Then they are also our friends. But friends are not enough usually.

For most of our lives, our most important attachment figure, the one most vital for our wellbeing, is our lover. We can only be as happy as our love relationship is.

Adult romantic love is an attachment bond, just like the one between mother and child. Our inborn need to depend on another 'precious-for-us' human being, starts at conception, when the egg meets the sperm, and never goes away. Bowlby said that this emotional relationship need endures 'from cradle to grave.'

As we grow past adolescence, our attachment needs get transferred from our parent(s) and/or caregiver(s) to our partner. At every age, human beings habitually seek and maintain physical and emotional closeness with at least on particular irreplaceable other. **To be human is to need others, and this is no flaw or weakness.**

There is **good research to show that we are social creatures**, and that social relationships are the number one key to happiness.[1] Isolation on the contrary brings in general misery and depression. We have evolved as human beings to belong to a group, the so called 'village.' In fact, the most important relationship is usually with our loved one. Belonging makes us feel not alone in the world.

Belonging to someone makes us feel more secure. There is comfort into knowing we 'belong' to someone. We should be able to be self-sufficient if needed for a bit, but **life is better spent if we have a deep, strong relationship with someone we can trust, we can confide with, we can count on**.

These early patterns make us who we are as adults. Research shows that **about 50% of us are secure, 20% anxious, 25% percent avoidant, and the other 5% a mix of anxious and avoidant**. We are programmed from genetics and even more from our early experiences to act in a predetermined manner when it comes to our rapport with others as adults. When we meet someone, the secure person goes, "This is probably a good interesting person...," the avoidant goes, "I do not trust him, let's see what he wants, I'm not opening up..."

These relationship patterns – secure, anxious, avoidant – are also **influenced by our life experiences in early adulthood**. A secure person who is betrayed in a love relationship may become anxious, or avoidant, in future relationships. An anxious child may become more secure after a good relationship with a secure person. Research shows that on average, **one in four people change a bit their attachment style in a four-year period**.

Human beings usually start life in a secure manner. For nine months, they were taken care of by the placenta, by their mother, by a warm secure uterine environment that provided everything they needed. We have been bred to depend upon someone else, and to trust them.

As a high-risk obstetrician, I do know there are exceptions. Some pregnant people have opioid use disorder or use other illicit drugs, some do not eat properly, some suffer violence of all kinds, physical, mental, and others. A secure attachment starts in utero, and unfortunately some of us did not even get nine months of secure bliss.

Being a parent is by far the most important job in the world. I like to think being an obstetrical provider and helping pregnant people be the best parent they can be from the beginning, and preserve a secure environment for their kid from conception, is the second most important job of all!!

Let's delve more into the details of these adult attachment patterns, as I think understanding them well, and using this new knowledge, is so important to achieve love happiness.

There are at least a couple of key differences between child and adult attachment. A key difference is that adult bonds should be reciprocal. We cannot just pretend to receive love, as when we were children. It's time for us to give.

Another difference between a child and an adult is that our 'lover' and giver of secure attachment does not have to be physically next to us all the time when we are adults. As an example, the Dalai Lama conjures up images of his mother when he wants to stay calm and centered.

Throughout evolution, secure people were favored, as being attached to another human being clearly provided a survival advantage. Those who were with someone who truly cared about them survived, and then passed their preference to form intimate secure love bonds to their own kids. Being close to loved ones provided food, shelter, and security from danger (Figure 1), as well as love and psychological support.

Being loved and protected by another, makes us live longer and maintains us in better health (Table 2). In my book 'Happiness: the scientific path to achieving wellbeing,' social relationship are proven by research to be, with scientific data and evidence, the #1 key to happiness.[1]

Secure people are those **comfortable with who they are**. They share their feelings and dreams often on the first dates. They are not afraid to share their past experiences, their likes, their strengths and their shortcomings. They like the same **openness** from their partners. Secure people **seek intimacy**; they are not afraid of it. **They know they are worthy of love**.

Secure people can openly and sincerely discuss the most intimate issues with their partners. They are **not afraid to share their most inner emotions**. They share their past history, their present matters, their future dreams.

Secure people trust others. They are programmed, genetically and from the loving environment they grew up with, to expect their partners to be loving and responsive. They feel extremely **comfortable with intimacy and closeness**. They are relaxed in giving their lover immense powers. They are ok with being authentic, with no barriers.

Secure people find it hard to understand why someone would be anxious, or avoidant, regarding a love relationship. They are the ones you notice ending up with 'the wrong partner,' and sticking to that flawed relationship because they want to 'change' their partner.

They feel so secure internally that they **would like to convince their anxious partner to be more relaxed**, to trust their love and live a more serene life. Secure people pair up with avoidants in the hope, which they believe for years to be quite feasible, **to try to open up the hedgehog, to take out the thorns one by one**, to finally be the one to uncover some love below the rough repellent surface. Secure people at times are stubborn in their own positivity, completely **unaware others may be different than them**.

Secure people are **consistent, reliable, trustworthy**. There is little drama in their romantic relationships. They do not cause crises, rollercoasters, as for example anxious people may be used to. Their stable emotional being does not get too agitated in the face of a threat as with an anxious person. They are open to the world, they do not shut down to others as avoidants do.

Secure people are **positive**. They are not worried about negative thoughts such as danger, loss, and separation. They are not sensitive to the negative clues of the world; they avoid negativism to bring them down. They concentrate on love, hugs, and closeness, and **both consciously and unconsciously find it hard to understand others who are more negative**.

They are not sensitive to the negative issues in the world. They concentrate on the positive. It frustrates them somewhat when they find others who do not see the world with the same **rosy lenses** they wear.

When we feel safe and connected to others, we are **more open to new experiences, and more open to others' point of view, beliefs. Curiosity** comes out of a sense of safety; rigidity out of being vigilant to threats.

You might have met a secure person, and passed them by since **you thought they were boring. They do not play games. They do not play hard to get.** They know what they want, and that a love relationship is serious matter. They are thoughtful about what they say. They are calm, and so may seem unexciting to an anxious type, for example.

Some people believe that love should be drama. That love should be highs and lows. Do not let emotional unavailability – for example of an avoidant type – turn you on in search of a conquest of an impossible person.

True love likes **peace of mind**. Secure people know that **happiness is only true when shared**. What a wonderful concept!! Do not confuse the drama that comes from the tension that develops between people of different attachment styles, for passion.

Studies show that a secure attachment style is one of the best predictor of happiness in a relationship. **People with a secure attachment style report higher levels of satisfaction in a relationship than other attachment styles.**

Secure people, almost no matter who they are partnered with, maintain over time high levels of relationship satisfaction, commitment, and trust. Insecure people such as anxious ones and especially avoidants, over time report decreasing levels of relationship satisfaction, again almost no matter who their partner is.

A secure person, when paired with an anxious one, or an avoidant, somehow often manages to raise their insecure partner's level of satisfaction. Secure people are great **conflict busters**. They can be mentally flexible. They are effective communicators. They do not play games. They are quick to forgive, as they assume in their positivity that their partner's intentions are good.

Secure people **tend to see emotional intimacy and sex as one**. They are the ones who say, "I love you" just before they have an orgasm. They have much better sex when they are in love with their partner. They treat their partner like royalty, with **love and respect.** They believe the relationship can always be improved, even if in their eyes it is already pretty great. **They feel responsible for their partner's well-being**.

They therefore **believe that there are many potential partners out there for them**. They believe others too would be like them, open to closeness, and would be responsible to their needs. Secure people know they deserve to be loved and valued at all times. Game playing is soon a deal breaker for them.

As they are effective communicators, their partners are soon made aware of their needs. If the partner cannot meet their basic, most important needs, secure people may not stick around to fight a losing battle, especially if they are aware of attachment styles and the difficulty, often the impossibility, of changing the partners' insecure attachment style.

Secure people can get along with insecure styles only if they themselves stay in their secure style. The problem arises when the anxious or avoidant partner wants to make their secure partner as insecure as they are. Secure people can stay up with an insecure partner only if that insecure partner opens up, becomes able to have intimacy and closeness, and in brief becomes more secure as a result of being with a secure person.

Secure people are not only effective communicators, but also effective communication coaches. They are good at getting others to open up and talk about personal things. This is a trait I was often told I have. I do love to pry into people's lives and make them open up about their most important issues, which to me are the emotional ones.

Sometimes secure people, when inexperienced, continue to give the benefit of the doubt to their insecure partners and tolerate their

actions despite their partner's negative behavior. Tolerating the insecure partners' negative behavior brings the secure partner down though. It makes them feel defeated, deflated. Secure people do tend to forgive others' wrongdoing more than others. **They protect their partners from others' negative judgement**.

Which is nice. But **long-term, secure people will find it intolerable to be unable to break the insecure pattern in their partner**. Only **two options** then will remain: **break up the relationship**; or become avoidant too in the negative relationship, to protect themselves from the pain of failure. **These secure people do not understand that it's not them who have failed. It's just their pairing with an insecure person that is the issue**.

When couples disagree on the degree of closeness and intimacy desired in a relationship, the issue eventually begins to dominate the whole relationship, all of the dialogue.

Just because you can get along with someone does not mean that you have to. If you have tried for years to make things work, and you are still unhappy, beginning to get anxious and/or avoidant behaviors, it means you as a secure person should move on.

Too many secure people stay with an unloving, insecure partner, denying themselves the love happiness they deserve. In fact, these unhappy, originally secure people, deny someone else out there the love and closeness they yearn to give and receive. **There are many others out there who share your secure need for intimacy and closeness**.

The obvious **smart decision in these situations is to end the relationship**. Some secure people are unable to break such unhappy relationships, especially when this is a long-term, committed relationship, say also with kids. The secure person may even find the courage to leave, only to rebound back with their prior partner, too afraid of being alone without any closeness with anyone whatsoever.

A breakup can be survived. Some keys to surviving a breakup are: opening up to friends and to family members, and using their support; being honest with others, and in particular to ourselves; realizing people do not usually change they attachment style; writing down the reasons why you want to leave; knowing that the pain will pass, time heals all wounds, and there are probably millions of better partners out there for you.

Let yourself suffer for a while. Those who behave like an English lord after a breakup were not in love. I was depressed on the brink of suicide after a true love story ended. Focus on the fact that you'll be alone for a while. But that being afraid of being alone should not be the reason for you to stay in an unhappy relationship. Do not compromise your happiness for fear of being alone, of not finding the 'one.' You'll find the 'one' if you free yourself of the 'non-one' and open your heart to the love you want and deserve.

The relationship our parents had, has a major impact on what lovers we become as adults. Secure people usually have had the benefit of seeing their partners having a positive, emotionally strong love relationship, which made them believe in love. Anxious and avoidant individuals often had parents who divorced, or did not get along.

Anxious people are only as needy as their unmet needs. With a secure person who is constantly present near them, and showers them with love and reassurance, they do great, and might even become secure in their attachment. With an avoidant type, their anxious behaviors multiply, making it crazy for the avoidant who, the more they stonewall, the more they seek distance, the more they get attacked by their anxious partner with requests for closeness.

Anxious people can also be described as 'fusers.'[6] They have an apparently **insatiable need for closeness**. They might have been pushed away from their parents, who did not have the time and attention for them that they deserved and were longing for. Now they want to do things together with their partners all the time.

Anxious people are more attentive to even minor changes in others' emotional expressions, tone of voice, words and hidden meanings. They tend to jump to negative conclusions quickly, often misinterpreting other's emotional state and what they wanted to say. Once the anxious attachment system is activated, it is hard to turn it off. Prevention is better than cure.

Anxious people are **usually uneasy about their partner's commitment and thus are primed to view anything she does or says**

negatively. They are haunted by the specter of abandonment, and so try to control their lover as much as they can, **wanting to know each and every details of her moves**.

Anxious people are also those who may be more prone to obsessive passion. It is a function of insecurity. Some call this also not being 'in love,' but being 'lovesick,' as these persons think they need love too much, making the partner crazy and looking for air to breath from the obsessive behavior.

In a way, **there is nobody that has more to offer in a relationship than an anxious individual**. They strongly want emotional connection and closeness, in an extreme way. The anxious partner may use sex to achieve a sense of affirmation and as a barometer of attractiveness in the eyes of their mate.

Avoidants intensify anxious people's worries and feelings of inadequacy. Secure partner pacify anxious people's worries. Anxious people should not date avoidants. Anxious people need to identify avoidants early on, by their unkindness, but their refusal to get close, no matter how kind they might seem at times. You should understand whether someone can meet your needs *before* committing long-term. Anxious people have the most to offer in a love relationship if their hopes are well placed.

Studies have shown that a specific pattern of the **dopamine receptor DRD2 allele** is associated with the anxious attachment style. So some aspect of this behavior can be improved, but not completely changed.

The **avoidant** person is a hedgehog. They have enormous difficulty saying 'I love you.' They are **uncomfortable being close to others, usually both physically and emotionally**. They do not trust others in general, they **aim not to depend on anyone else**. They get nervous if anyone gets too close, or tries to get too close. They shun away from intimacy, from closeness in a relationship.

They think **the worst possible thing in life is to depend on another human being**. They were often taught while very young that they can only count on themselves. Or they learned it when they found themselves devoid of a close person who loved them.

Their belief in self-reliance stemmed from their need to avoid closeness and intimacy with others, as they do not trust others, having been 'burned' in love while children. **Loving another person has become for them far too risky emotionally. They cannot go through that unbearable pain again**.

It is quite ok for them to be '**self-reliant**,' to be able to survive alone if and when needed. Avoidants even make the next step towards thinking they can be completely independent, and never need others, really. They **concentrate therefore only on their self**. They concentrate only on their needs, and **cannot see the need of others**. Studies show that avoidant individuals are less accurate than secure or anxious individuals at perceiving their partners' thoughts and feelings.

They prevent themselves (and the person who loves them) from the joy of feeling part of something bigger than themselves. They have also been called 'isolaters.' They need a lot of space, and they need to push others away.

'**Needing' someone else to be happy is seen as weak by avoidants, and disgusts them**. They accuse their partners of being too demanding. They somehow learned as children to shun pleasure. They learned that pleasure and intimacy are bad, to be avoided.

Studies on avoidants confirm they are **quick to think negatively about their partners**. They tend to see the **glass half-empty** instead of half-full when it comes to their partner. Avoidants tend to remember the worst of their partners. There is scientific evidence to show that people with an avoidant attachment style tend to be **less happy and satisfied** in their relationships.

Avoidants see their partners as needy and overly dependent. They despise others for being clingy; this is a major element on how they see relationships. They see themselves as not needing the partner, really.

Interestingly, good scientific research has proven that avoidants do have attachments needs. But **they actively suppress these emotional innate needs**. Studies have shown that avoidants use their 'free spirit,' 'I-do-not-depend-on-anyone' stance and public attitude as a **defensive stand**.

The avoidants still have the 'attachment' machinery on, but they just try to ignore it, to turn it off. **They also, like anyone else, need others, despite their vehemently denying so.** Stressful life events such as divorce, other traumas, often can break the avoidant's defenses, and make them appear and behave just like people with an anxious attachment style.

Avoidants find it difficult not to see flaws in their partner. The avoidant maintains mental distance, and does not allow their partner into their lives. They use '**deactivating' strategies**, i.e. behaviors and thoughts meant to squelch intimacy, to avoid closeness.

Examples of **deactivating** strategies are focusing on small imperfection of the partner; not saying 'I love you;' not calling for days even after a great date; avoiding physical closeness, such laying close in the same bed; not wanting to have sex.

Avoidant people blame external circumstance for their being unhappy with love: having the wrong partner, not finding the 'one,' the wrong timing. **They do not look inside themselves for the reason for their dissatisfaction. They never see themselves as even the slightest part of the problem.**

Avoidants idealize a life of self-sufficiency, and **look down upon dependency. These are lonesome travelers.** They tend to **suppress their emotions.** They make their partner feel alone even when in a supposed relationship. Studies show that people with an avoidant attachment style tend to be less happy, and less satisfied with their relationships. They feel in 'jail time' if people seek closeness. They are free spirits.

Avoidants have usually been **children exposed to loss of attachment.** They went to the four phases of, 1. Anger and protest; 2. Clinging and seeking; 3. Depression and despair; and 4. Detachment. Once they hit detachment, it's hard to change from the attitude of just not being able to trust someone else to be close ever again.

Studies have shown a specific pattern of the **serotonin 5-HT1A receptor allele** is associated with the avoidant attachment style. So again some aspect of this behavior can be improved, but not completely changed.

You have probably dated avoidant people. They tend to be more available in the dating pool. This is because avoidants end their relationships more often; and because secure people instead tend to take a long time to reappear, if at all, in the dating pool.

People who have avoidants as partners live in a chronic state of dissatisfaction. The amount of intimacy wanted by the secure or by the anxious partner is never given by the avoidant. The avoidant's partner soon starts to go crazy, and eventually helpless and defeated.

Why are people attracted to avoidant persons? One reason could be to resolve a childhood frustration with an avoidant parent. We unconsciously project our pain with having had a parent who did not love us the way we would have wanted, who was not close enough, and now **we seek a partner with similar characteristics, to try and solve the old issue, and 'convert' the partner from avoidant to cuddly and loving**.

There are actually research data that **we do try to match with a partner with the traits of our parents, and often we match up more with parents' negative than positive traits**. For example, if we had a distant father who did not give us emotional or physical warmth, we tend to seek a similar pattern, and then try to convert him to a warmer cuddly person. This obviously might not work well at all. Our childhood longings might become life-long. Same for an abusive father and then partner.

Sadly, in a US study, when men with a history of angina and high blood pressure were asked, "Does your wife show her love?" those who answered "No" suffered almost twice as many episodes of angina during the next five years as those who replied "Yes."[10]

Women who view their relationships as strained and have regularly hostile interactions with their partners are more likely to have high blood pressure and high levels of stress hormones compared to women in happy relationships where they feel loved by a secure partner.

Avoidants feel independent and powerful to the extent that their partner feels needy and incapable. This is one of the reasons **avoidants hardly ever date each other**. The anxious partner often just needs to give in to the avoidant's rules, to her stronger personality.

When our partner is unable to meet our basic attachment needs, we experience a chronic sense of loss, tension. Our immune system weakens. We get sick with viruses and other diseases. Our partners profoundly affect our ability to thrive in the world. They influence how we feel about ourselves; they influence the degree to which we believe in ourselves; they influence whether we will attempt to follow our hopes and dreams.

Our partner's love is like the wings we fly with. Without wings, we do not fly. Once we realize we are not loved, or not loved in a way we enjoy, we crumble back to earth hurt and wounded. Having a partner who is not always supportive and securely attached to us, stunts our emotional being, compromises our health.

So one must realize that **certain ongoing struggles with the relationship are not because either of you are crazy, but because your relations has a built-in clash that is not going to go away**.

One of the saddest parts is that **someone who does not love you makes you feel like your character is just weak** to need all that love. They do not comprehend how someone is so needy for love. The person who does not love, finds in the other lack of constancy, doubts, anxieties, exaggerations, probably even untruthfulness, as they cannot comprehend their need to feel loved.

It's one thing to accuse one singular behavior. It's another to find a major character flaw in the partner. Bearing one's own need to be loved is seem as a flaw. Feelings are seen as a sign of childishness, naivety. The avoidant person now, if allowed to stay in the relationship, gets enormous power on the loving partner.

The loving partner is desperate, and thinks he is the culprit of all problems. All interactions depend on the avoidant, who controls every aspect of the relationship. The loving partner can only survive by false hope.

They learn to be thankful for what their partner does do, and to overlook what he or she does not do. These secure people let go of their dreams. They compromise. They are often not aware **the avoidant does not compromise; only they do**. These secure people report much lower level of satisfaction in the relationship.

Some would view such unhappy secure people as pathetic. They could be judged as deserving the mistreatment they are unable to get out of. They put up with **their partners finding a problem in everything in their lives**.

Such non-reciprocal relationship can, even when ended, have **lifelong consequences for the non-avoidant partner who was truly in love**. That partner may get petrified in a perennial state of believing to be not worth of love. To be too demanding, too difficult, too immature.

Fighting a losing battle is frustrating. The secure partner does try to learn to accept him the way he is. But it feels like this means she would have to become someone else. That she would be another person in her own body. That for every second of her life, she could not have what she most craves, closeness and intimacy.

Yes, **some secure people stay with avoidants for a lifetime**. Millions of such couples have celebrated 50, 60, 70+ years together. The secure partner of an avoidant person can only stay in by stopping any demands for closeness and intimacy. By giving up on what they thought was most important for them; as important as water and food. They start doing things with others. They may develop another parallel life. They may cheat with others seeking what the avoidant cannot give them.

Cheating done by secure people is the symptom of their failed relationship, of the **emptiness of emotions** they feel with their official partner. The aridity at home makes the one partner who still believes in romantic love look elsewhere for what she knows is essential like water for her survival.

Society is too quick to gossip superficially at cheating, without truly looking into the reasons for the cheating. It is like blaming someone for having a disease, without trying to find the cause and then the proper cure. The cause is an unhappy relationship, and the cure is not cheating, but usually divorce and finding a more suitable partner.

The gaps between anxious/avoidant or secure/avoidant **may become wider with time**. This is because as the secure or anxious partner seeks more intimacy from the avoidant, the avoidant tends to become more and more hostile, more and more distant, avoiding these intimacy conversations all together as meaningless and superfluous.

The **way forward** for avoidants is to realize their attachment style, and therefore acknowledge their need for space. When things get too close, they should explain to their partner that any move to more closeness, emotional or physical, makes them uncomfortable. They should reassure their companion that it's not her who is unattractive or boring or dumb.

Avoidants should seek time alone, and explain to their partner this is an important need for them; and that it has nothing to do with the relationship. In any relationship, with anyone, the avoidant needs freedom. **His partner can be reassured that this has nothing to do with them**.

It's important you realize if you are dating an avoidant. **If you dropped your seed on a rock, it's the rock, not you, that prevented it from growing**. It's just that you don't fit each other, you are too different, and the rock will stay a rock and prevent you always, just like rocks do, from getting in and grow your seeds of love. Your seeds will die. You will emotionally die if you still hope the rock will let the love seeds grow.

It's really important to know who you are (Table 4). To know what your needs are. If you are anxious, you should probably steer clear of an avoidant person. Or at least go into that relationship knowing what you can expect, and knowing what you will not get, e.g. frequent love reassurance. The avoidant just cannot provide that.

The **importance of being attached to someone was dramatically confirmed** by Harry Harlow, a psychologist at the University of Wisconsin. What he called as '**contact comfort**' was demonstrated by his research with **monkeys who had been separated from their mothers at birth**.

The isolated monkey infants were so hungry for connection that when given the choice between a 'mother' made out of wire who dispensed food and a soft-cloth 'mother' without food, they would chose the squashy rag mother almost every time.

Physically healthy infant primates who were separated from their mothers during the first year of life grew into socially crippled adults. The monkeys failed to develop the ability to solve problems or understand the social clues of others. They became depressed, self-destructive, and unable to mate.

So many factors contribute to what our attachment style is. There seem to be three strongest factors, as per research so far, that determine our attachment style.

First, our DNA.

Second, the way our parents brought us up, the love attachment style we received from them, and what we saw around us, especially in the house we were brought up in. The strength of our bonds to our mother at age 1, for example, has been shown in studies to correlate to how good we are at dealing with romantic emotions and resolving conflicts in our romantic relationships at age 21!

Third, our attachment style is influenced by **our romantic experiences as adults, especially young adults**.

Interestingly, 70-75% of adults remain consistently in the same attachment category throughout their life, from childhood to senility. About **25-30% of people report a change in their attachment style at some point in their life**. Example would be an anxious person supported by a secure partner. Or a secure person attracted to avoidants, who eventually gives up on the hope of making others as positive and happy as they thought they were.

It's key to believe that some change is possible. Neuronal reorganization is possible, but it requires lots of work. For example, if we blind ourselves, after a couple of days our senses of hearing and touch get enhanced. Falling in love, and having children, are the two events most likely to cause the most changes in our brains.

I can easily categorize people very close to me as secure, anxious, or attached. One of my close relatives was '**the second, less loved sister**,' while her sister was the apple of her mother's eyes. Feeling 'second best' from your own mother, since the start of life, makes this person anxious in her adult love relationships. "Will I be loved truly? Deeply? Or will I be 'second' again and again, not a priority for the person I love?"

In the wonderful love relationship she has developed with a secure husband, she needs him to prove his love over and over. After 40 years of a great marriage, she still feels anxious at times that she loves him more than he loves her, and that she is not sure he really loves her.

Often there is nothing the partner is doing wrong; it's just that the anxious lover needs nearly constant reassurance of truly being loved, given the scars left from parental relationships, or past partnerships.

Another person I know was **not the preferred kid by her mother**. Her brother was clearly, always, the preferred one. She was left with the 'crumbles' of her mother's love. She was so hurt, that she **became avoidant**. She would not seek love. Being an attractive person, she attracted boys' attention, which she often shunned. Even when with people she really liked, once things got too close, she would break the relationship.

Avoidant people begin to devalue their partner when things get too close, using this 'cold shoulder' approach to distance the partner from themselves. After a five year relationship, with official engagement and plan to marry, another woman told her partner two months before the wedding that she was not sure about getting married. "**We are doing fine as is, why get married?**"

The knowledge of attachment patterns helped me see prior relationships in a better, even sometimes new, light. My mother treated me with secure love. Never for a second I thought she would not be there for me. I know she would give everything, including her own life, for my health and wellbeing.

I should have not gone out with girlfriends who were avoidant. I was blinded by good looks, a grave mistake. I really need to love and to be loved, to feel like I can count on the affection of the person next to me. Why try to be loved by someone who cannot provide it? It's actually not even their fault that they are avoidant.

I should have figured out my needs for someone secure much earlier in my life. In fact, an anxious person would have been ok too, as I hope I can provide a secure attachment, and benefit from the constant need of my anxious partner for love and affection and affirmation.

In the same vein, I have friends who have a tremendous need for love and affection, and instead have been for decades with avoidant partners. Why do they continue like this? Why the pain?

It's important to use these attachment-pattern knowledge to **choose well our long-term partner**, and to also learn what we can expect from our partner. Interesting, there are research studies which show that anxious women are more likely to date avoidant men. And that avoidant individuals prefer anxious people. This may happen because each reaffirms the other's beliefs about themselves.

Anxious people feel confirmed in their belief that they need more reassurance than they get. It might be that they became anxious because of an avoidant parent, and so they feel used and somehow uncomfortably familiar with that situational relationship. Similarly, the avoidant's self-perception of being strong and independent and so sought for those qualities, is confirmed.

One of the many beauties I find in these data-driven facts, is that **the more dependent people are towards a loved one, the more independent they become**. I am living proof of this. I am and have always been so secure of my mother's love, that I was strong enough to move to another continent when I was 19 years old, all by myself.

My mother's love was secure, her support even from far unwavering and incorporated into my soul. Being dependent on my mother's love, made me independent enough to take on the world.

When I felt not loved and emotionally protected by my partner, I fell into **depression**. My maternal side of the family is full of depression, and my mother's uncle committed suicide. I also wanted to jump out of the window.

I felt alone, unloved, desperately unable to love the person I wanted to love given the **rejection** I was feeling. Rejection and emotional exclusion trigger the same circuits in the same part of the brain, the anterior cingulate, **as physical pain**.

I did not want to believe our relationship was the reason of my unhappiness. Thanks to therapy and the research I did for this book, I understand this former partner is just different from me in attachment style. She does not enjoy intimacy and closeness in the same way as I do.

I have stopped therapy and prescription-medicine help given the deep emotional connection I now share with my wife, who proves her love daily, in fact every minute. I depend on her love, I am secure in her love, and so I can independently and courageously take on the whole world.

This is an important fact. **Many feel it's best to not count on anyone; to be able to go through life without needing another person's love. The scientific data say that is absolutely wrong. The more you depend and benefit from someone's love, the more you can achieve independently.**

The fact that a person's success depends on their partner's support, is absolutely based on the scientific evidence. It is erroneous to believe that we should be emotionally self-sufficient. Those who scorn intimacy, closeness, and dependency, have been shown to be the most miserable and unhappy among us.

We are not made to be self-sufficient! Emotional dependency is not immature or pathological; it is our greatest strength!! In fact, **being dependent makes us more independent.** Two lovers find their **blood pressure, heart rate, respiratory rate, hormones, being similar, healthy, in synchronous harmony.**

A corollary is that a good partner should understand the tremendous impact he has on his significant other. As the partner depends on us, a reprimand, physical or emotional absence, or distance, will cause tremendous angst. This is not to say arguing should not occur. But **the focus should be on not harming a soul which depends on us to be happy and content.**

Going back full circle, and knowing now what you just learned, please **be a good parent when you are ready to be one. Distance between parent and child should be minimal.** Physical and emotional affection should be doled out to children in massive amounts.

I used to think that my ex-wife spending two hours in bed with grown up children while putting them to bed would make our sons weak; I was wrong, and I thank her for having made them into secure adults.

The greatest gift a parent can give to her child – and a partner has to give to his lover – is emotionally attuned attention and timely responsiveness.

The 5 love languages

All happiness and unhappiness solely depend upon the quality of the object to which we are attached by love.
Baruch Espinosa

The **5 love languages, as developed by Gary Chapman,**[4] changed my life. I read these books when a past relationship had begun to struggle. Chapman's arguments were to me a **revelation**.

The 5 love languages (Table 5) are:

- Words of affirmation
- Gifts
- Acts of service
- Quality time
- Physical touch

Like with happiness, intelligence, body habitus, and so many other human traits, about **50% of love languages are inherited genetically**. One's nerve endings may be more or less prone to be stimulated by physical touch. The altruism of acts of kindness and gifts is often innate.

Some of us feel connected to spend quality time together with another person we enjoy being with, some of us instead are more independent and introspective. I remember a middle school classmate of mine who would praise everyone. And she did it with such apparent ease and sincerity. She was born to give words of affirmation, and even the critical puberty time did not darken her flattering attitude.

You probably do not 'speak' all five love languages well. Thankfully, **all love languages can be learned, and perfected, over time**. We might not be born with physical touch, but a mother or father who cuddles us all the time may make us more prone to closeness. We might not be prone to give gifts, but having a sibling who is, may teach us with repeated examples the kindness of receiving, and even more of giving, a gift.

In fact Chapman stresses the fact that **we should speak all 5 love languages**. He states that we should be proficient in all 5. And that we should become masters at receiving love in each of the 5 languages, and even more importantly become masters at giving love in all 5 forms. This is a **fundamental key to love happiness**.

How many couples have you heard when one partner complains, "He never helps me with house chores. If he truly loved me, he would help me clean the dishes and loading the dishwasher. He would volunteer to do the laundry once in a while. He never does. He keeps repeating he loves me, but to me words are cheap. I'd much rather he do the grocery shopping, than tell me how much he loves me, or buy me flowers."

In this relationship, she loves by acts of kindness. He loves by words of affirmation, and gifts. Like a Russian and an Arab trying to communicate and get along, with no translator available. It's never going to work, unless both make an effort to learn each other's languages of love.

Let me describe the love languages. Let's start with **physical touch**. **Simply holding the hand of a loved one**, our mother when young or our lover when adults, can affect us profoundly. Women having an MRI were told in a study that **when a red light came on, they might or might not get a small electric shock** to their feet.

The stress was high in their brain when this electric shock was given, as seen in the functional MRIs. But **when their husbands held they hands**, the patient registered less stress, and when the electric shock occurred, they had less pain. This effect, moreover, was noticeably stronger in the happier relationships, the ones in which partners scored high on measures of satisfaction.

Words of affirmation are either genetically engrained, or can also be learned in an environment, like the one I grew up in, that is pleasant, joyful, positive. Some of us grew up as children who heard routinely affirming words, words of praise, of encouragement.

Children who have as a top love language words of affirmation, feel unloved by their partners, and their friends, without praise, compliments. Some people, either genetically or because of how their parents brought them up, do not praise or compliment others. But this is a skill, like the other love languages, that can be learned even as adults.

Acts of kindness is the ultimate altruistic love language. Jesus washing the feet of his disciples was definitively an act of kindness. Serving others is one of the noblest virtues one can have. **The calling to assist someone else** is as close to heaven as we get on this earth.

'**To give is better than to receive**' is what acts of kindness is all about. Mother Theresa is what I think about when I think of acts of kindness. And also my former mother-in-law, who would gift me the sweater, or the meal, she knew I liked. Expecting nothing in return. Helping others is perhaps the most universally accepted expression of love.

It's also important not to keep score. One does not load the dishwasher in the hope the other does the laundry tomorrow. One should do the dishwasher as a selfless act of kindness to her partner. To generate positive feelings in general for the relationship. To fill the love happiness tank. If you find yourself keeping score, that will be an area of tension between you two.

Giving and receiving gifts is another love language. A gift is a tangible object that say, "I was thinking about you. I wanted you to have this. You had told me you liked it, and I remembered it. It's because I love you." A gift is altruistic love. A gift made for love does not expect anything in return. A gift is given without strings attached.

Quality time means togetherness. These people love by wanting to spend time with each other. Uninterrupted time to talk, quietly, softly, one-on-one, with no distractions. A walk on the beach together. Watching the sunset. Empathic listening is an awesome medication for our partner.

Let's make these love languages clearer by reviewing some practical examples. An illustration of quality time is that one of the colleagues I most admire, takes a one, one-and-a-half hour **walk in the evening with his wife every day**. He says that's one of the major keys to the success of his >35 years marriage.

We want focused attention. From the person we trust the most. We need precious moments to unwind the stresses from work to our trusted confidante, our partner. And we need to continue to know the intimacies

56

of our partner's inner self and brain as he opens up his most inner feelings to us in quality minutes.

People who have quality time as one of their top languages want a partner who is able to listen. Who can have the time, and the patience, to hear worries, fears, random thoughts, feelings, moods. Without actually judging back. Quality time wants just a shoulder to lean on, an ear to speak to, a 'yes yes,' or 'uhm' once in a while, testifying we are paying attention.

Quality time is, generally, the language of those of us who want the deeper emotional connection. Who truly have few boundaries with their partners, and sincerely want to be an active, involved part of the other's life.

Deep attentive listening, uninterrupted, is what quality time is most about. Observing each other body language, as 70% of communication is non-verbal, is very helpful. Eye contact makes quality time even more profound. More than a solution to a problem, the person who loves quality time might expect from the person questions, which might pry the soul and let the person solve the issue by herself.

I myself have this strong feeling of needing to express my love in a bodily way. And **I express it most naturally with my two top love languages, physical touch, and words of affirmation.** I need to love in these languages almost more than I need to be loved with them. I do feel loved with the same love languages, when I am hugged, caressed, when we are cuddling, loving each other with touch and compliments.

May be this is really what we fall in love for: the way the other person allows us to love them and loves us. For me, I clearly long for **a love similar to how my mother loved me.** This is not easy to admit for an Italian who can easily be labeled as 'mammone.' The truth for me, after all these years, is that genetically **I was born to touch and to be touched. And to give and receive praise.** These two love languages come natural to me. I was born this way. It's in my DNA.

Then **I was exposed to my mother's love.** She loved me, and loves me still, unconditionally. With caressing and touching, and with **continuous praise**, such as "How could have I made such a wonderful son," "You can achieve whatever you want in life," etc. She nicknamed me 'Passione' since I was a little boy. She deluged me with continuous physical contact. And with endless commendations.

My sister speaks the gift love language well. She gives the perfect thoughtful gift all the time. I never did speak this language that well. My former mother-in-law and ex-wife are great at acts of kindness; world-class. Replacing one's toothpaste. Making dinner. Doing laundry.

I enjoy quality time a lot, but I have learned it overtime, once I realized the importance of social relationship, and that work should not be the end-all, despite what my father pushed for.

My father's love I felt much less than my mother's. He just wanted me to work, study, work. He shook my hand, did not hug me. He almost never gave a compliment. I did not feel his love. Since he was very smart, he changed later in life.

After I turned 40-45, he began praising me. Complimenting me. Even the occasional hug (one big one when I was 19 as I thanked him for the car he bought for me – one of the best photos in my life).

Interestingly, **I married first someone like my dad**. She did not compliment me. I worked hard to 'earn' her love. She would not tell me spontaneously "I love you," or praise me for something I did. I could not feel her love. Instead, I felt distance. Even if my shampoo would always be replenished on time. We were just so different. Nothing wrong with either of us. Just very different.

I probably should have married – and did eventually – someone like my mom. Federica compliments me all the time. Calls me 'Amore,' 'Tesoro,' and externalizes her love constantly. I feel her love. I feel it strong, passionate. It is the bright ray of sunshine which gets me through the day. Like my mother's love did when I was younger.

In part what we are looking for in love is familiarity. We are looking to re-create the love feeling we had as children in our adult relationship. My mother was physically cuddling and verbally praising; I need those traits in my partner as an adult.

My father was serious, hard-working and a reassuring figure; my sister found those traits in her husband. Some have parental traits they want to avoid in a partner, and so they are drawn to people who are non-violent, who do not scream, who are able to hold down a job responsibly.

For example, regarding acts of kindness, **doing the laundry for me does not make me feel loved that much. You can buy someone to clean up, cook, do laundry**. You cannot (and should not) buy someone to physically touch you. I know some of you might not think this way. I'm just giving my honest personal opinion, based on research data.

The important issue is to **take a love language questionnaire** (https://5lovelanguages.com/quizzes/love-language), and be ready to learn to love your partner the way she wants to be loved. Because then your partner is more likely to go to great efforts to love you the way you want to be loved.

Knowledge of love languages is a must in love relationships. And **this knowledge is also very helpful in life in general**. Even at work, some people like to be hugged, some like to be complimented, some other like to be brought coffee. Knowing what others appreciate can make you a lot more successful at work, and in life in general.

Love requires effort. The choice to love is the choice to **take the initiative**. To learn your love languages. To learn your partner's love languages. Listen, really listen. Observe. Notice when he smiles. When his eyes glitter. What did you just do? That's the love language he appreciates.

Love so much as to learn a love language you do not speak yet. You were not born with. Your parents did not teach you. A love language you might not even think it's that important. But a love language without receiving which your partner won't know you love her.

Gabriel García Márquez said that **the fact that one person doesn't love you the way you'd want, does not mean that he/she doesn't love you with all himself**. Nonetheless, we should really strive to learn all the love languages, both in how to give them, and in how to receive them.

Once you learn how you like to be loved, and how your partner likes to loved, then purposely love each other so to make each other happy. **Love stimulates love**. A love language you do not know, you do not practice, can be learned.

For example, if you are not yet a physical touch person, next time you see your parents, and you know they are physical touch persons, give them a hug. If your partner likes gifts, set an alarm to buy them one: it's

59

easy with the internet to even just buy one gift online if you do not like shopping.

You often need to rewire your thinking to learn the importance of a love language you do not practice yet. Perhaps your dad is always asking you to do things for him. And you have always found that annoying. Even if he always did lots of things for you. You must understand your dad is **actually just asking you to love him**. His love language is acts of service.

Your partner wants you to do laundry. You'd rather hire someone to do that. Or teach the kids to help out. But your partner needs *you* to do the laundry yourself. She feels loved if you do the laundry. You think that's crazy. But actually she is just asking to be loved with a love language she appreciates. No quality time or words of affirmation will do if her main love language is acts of service.

When our partner loves us with our top love language(s), we feel a warmth in our hearts. We are drawn to our partner emotionally. We want to reciprocate the love, the kindness of making us feel so loved. We feel high. We have high, positive regard for them. Our bond with them deepens, gets stronger.

It is **scientifically proven that in relationships in which both partners have similar love languages, e.g. the top two are quality time and acts of kindness for both, love is deeper, easier, and lasts longe**r. Life is a lot more serene if love languages are similar, and a bit more work if love languages differ.

Going back to our first chapter, and the fact that **love is wanting to make the other person happy,** speaking their love language gives our partner the **deep emotional sensation of feeling loved**. He would say, "I feel loved by my partner;" and "My partner really cares about me." It's the ultimate love happiness.

Before committing to each other 'forever,' it is a *must* to learn your love languages, and those of your partner. Do not marry until you have learned to speak each other's love languages well, early in the relationship. It will save you a lot of heartache. **Keep you love tank full** by speaking the love languages your partner most appreciates. Any time you do speak the love language your partner adores, you'll pour into the love tank.

We are all very different

In your subconscious you have an image of a certain kind of person that attracts you. Once you see this kind of person, you fall in love. But falling in love does not have anything to do with true love. True love requires lots of time and understanding. They say love is blind. Love can see very well, in fact it has the best eyesight in the world for the tiniest aspects of your spouse.

Anthony De Mello

Perhaps God wants that you meet many persons who are not right for you so that, once you meet the right one, you'd be grateful.

Gabriel García Márquez

In my youth, I considered people as very similar to each other. Indeed, you and I and all humans share 99.99% of the same DNA. Studying, reading, experiencing life by meeting so many people, I've discovered we are indeed so different.

I've reviewed already that there are 3 different attachment styles: secure, anxious and avoidant (Table 3). And that there are 5 different love languages (Table 5). Just with these characteristics, you can get 15 different types of people.

In terms of personality types, there are 16 different ones (https://www.16personalities.com/free-personality-test). People can also have 34 different strengths (https://store.gallup.com/p/en-us/10003/cliftonstrengths-34). Just these 4 possible ways to examine who we are and what we like, give 8,160 different combinations.

Even more importantly, there are at least 9 essential love elements we have or not have in different degrees (Table 6), and 12 factors associated with a successful long-term relationship (Table 7) at which we might excel or be terrible at. Now the possible combinations of different humans reaches 881,280. We are all very different, as the list of characteristics we might differ in is obviously even longer.

Interestingly, none of these 79 personal characteristics has to do with physical appearance. Having a physical **identikit** for a lover is

61

detrimental. **Please do not choose based on looks; external factors; fame; fortune; shoes. Choose in terms of values, attitude** (Tables 6, 7). Our societies bombard us with thin models. They are some of the unhappiest humans.[1]

The key is to accept that these character differences are real. And then study exactly who we are and what fits best for us as a partner in terms of these features:

1. Attachment styles (Table 3)
2. Love languages (Table 5)
3. Essential love elements (Table 6)
4. Factors associated with a successful long-term relationship (Table 7)

Without this detailed knowledge, we are bound to fail in finding the right partner. We can't just chose randomly, and expect love happiness if we just try hard enough. Often the identikit in our mind comes from what our parents, friends, culture say we should go for. Not what *you* like, and need. Without the knowledge of what you like (Tables 3,5,6,7), the person you least fit with, might become your lifemate.

Try to create an **imago of a possible partner** early in your adult life based on character qualities. We do use the imago of an ideal partner to screen people we meet. At first, we need to be open with anyone. If you imago involves a nice behind, that's what you'll fall for. Long-term, it will pay a lot more in term of love happiness to seek people with character traits you desire and admire (Table 6). Love happiness will continue to be uncommon unless you follow these principles.

A love relationship begins far earlier than when two people meet. It begins first instead with the ideas we form in our head of what our ideal soulmate and our ideal love happiness should be.

Should you marry someone similar to you, or someone different? The French say, "Qui se resemble s'assemble," i.e. "Those who are similar get together." Other cultures state that opposites attract, and therefore end up together. Science seems to show that **some main character traits you deem highly important should be similar between you and your partner**.

A recent meta-analysis (summary) of studies showed no evidence that opposites attract, and instead much evidence that **people pair as couples with individuals who are similar to them.**[10] Traits such as political and religious attitudes, level of education, and certain measures of IQ showed particularly high correlations.

Traits surrounding substance use also showed high correlations, with heavy drinkers, smokers, and teetotalers tending to strongly pair with those who share similar traits. Traits like height and weight, medical conditions, and personality showed much lower but still positive correlations.

Couples could share traits for a variety of reasons, including growing up in a similar area. Some people might simply be attracted to those who are alike to them in appearance, and some couples grow more similar in character the longer they stay in the relationship.

Research show in general we look for an imago match with our opposite sex parent. Someone so similar to our parent that our unconscious mind has them fused. Importantly, **we need to match important traits, positive traits, not unimportant, and/or negative traits**.

If our partner has the same negative traits of our childhood caretaker, they are the least likely to make us love happy. For example, if one had a parent who was not warm and did not share affection by physical touch, one might as an adult crave to pair up with someone who is also low in physical touch.

The problem is that there is a low chance that the partner will change. One will become instead even more frustrated and unhappy as now as an adult he has recreated the unloving relationship he had as a child. Please do not heal your childhood wounds this way. In this example, one should chose instead a partner already with high physical touch affection.

A big misconception many humans have is that everyone has the same capacity for intimacy. Our culture makes us believe that every person can fall deeply in love – well, this might be true for most people. And that when this happens, this love will transform him into a different person – this is false, and usually does not happen!

The movies at times make us believe that once in love, once married, anyone can change and treat her spouse like royalty. This is not true!! **Mismatched attachments styles can lead to a great deal of unhappiness in relationships, even for people who love each other deeply**.

The fact is that people instead are very different, each with a different capacity for intimacy. Once in love, some seek closeness, some in fact still need independence and distance. This can cause a lot of unhappiness, and miscomprehension. **It's really important to understand these different attachment styles**. Secure people for example in general report much happier relationships when paired with another secure person.

Do not accept blatant disregards for your emotions. Your emotions are right. They are who you are. A true caring partner views as his responsibility to ensure the other's emotional well-being.

What is insane to someone, might be a godsend for another. Some long for neatness; some despise it. Some like physical touch; I know so many people who prefer physical distance. There is nothing wrong with any of these preferences. The important issue is to understand what we prefer, and to then pick partners based on those preferences.

If we like neatness, and our partner is messy, there is nothing wrong with either us or them. We need to just decide if neat/messy is a necessary trait for us to be happy with our partner or not. But there is no need to insult our partner because of who and how they are.

In fact, **it's ok for each of us to be different, corky, somewhat insane in some ways**. It is instead absurd, when we recognize traits in our partner that do not fit our preferences, to blame them. **We cannot get angry at them for being who they are**. We often forgive strangers much more than we forgive our partners.

If we truly love someone, there should be limited, if any, talk of wanting him or her to change much. A little may be, but not much. Instead we expect our partner to be in every aspect like ourselves. We desire them to 'want what we want' and 'feel the way we feel.' We mistakenly assume that if our partner truly loves us, they will react and behave in certain ways – the ways we react and behave when we love someone.[12]

True long-term love involves an **acceptance** of a partner's whole being, including the parts we do not 'love' so much. **Love is based on admiration for strengths, and compassion for weaknesses.** To pretend that the other changes, leads to insults, our partner's wounded pride, as she grows ever more defensive and hurt.

Positive feedback, calling attention to faults, letting each other critiques one another, with positive intentions and compromise, is part of long-term love. We should help our partner become a better version of himself, and let ourselves be critiqued to continue to grow and improve. But we must stop when this reaches a limit and causes anger.

Famously, in terms of being different, John Gray divided us in Martians – Men, and Venusians – Women.[13] Gender lines are thankfully much more fluid compared to when this was written, and LGBTQIA+ can be Martians, Venusians, or a mix. And men can be Venusians, as well as women Martians. The framework it's still helpful to review just how different we all can be.

For example for many, in particular **men** in past generations, sense of self is defined through his ability to achieve results. Often he values power, competency, efficacy, and achievement. Getting compliments for his achievements feels great to him.

Many men are motivated when they feel needed because of some special skill they have. Not to be needed is a slow death for a man. He needs to feel appreciated, trusted, and accepted. He actually needs desperately to be loved.

Many of us, in particular **women, want to be listened to** instead. Love can be shown in this case by hearing out with empathy and interest, and being just supportive, without necessarily offering solutions. Venusians are concerned with living together in harmony, community, and loving cooperation. Relationships are more important than work and technology. The number one complain women have in a relationship is that they don't feel heard.

Women are motivated when they feel cherished, when they feel supported, when they feel not alone in their struggles. What she needs most if for someone to listen. Some Venusians for centuries gave and gave, but deep inside they did not feel worthy of receiving. They hoped that by giving, they would become more worthy of receiving.

These women obviously should not expect themselves to give more and receive less; their partner may actually give more if he receives less. Truth is, it's best for one partner to make a positive change and the other to follow.

Martians feel good when they achieve goals and success. They may not share as much their feelings. They do not have, like Venusians, a master in psychology and extra training in counseling. Martians are goal oriented, while Venusians are relationship oriented. So for example **a sign of great love by a Martian is to offer help and assistance to a Venusian without being asked**.

Instead **sometimes for a woman to offer help to man, can backfire, as some men may feel incompetent, weak, or even unloved** when helped in something they think they can and/or should do by themselves. Generally speaking, when a woman offers unsolicited advice or tries to 'help' a man, she has no idea of how critical or unloving she might sound to him.

Moreover, **it is difficult for a man to listen to a woman when she is unhappy or disappointed, because he feels like a failure**. Women should perhaps understand at times that they cannot expect hours being listened to by the same person always. Sometimes a best friend, a sister, a mother, can also act as someone who can listen to our struggles. Certainly the most important ears remain those of her partner. It's just impossible to pretend the same empathy from a person who is not as empathic as they are. Nonetheless, their partner should try his hardest.

Different planets, indeed.

A big difference in people is **how each of us reacts to stress**. Some may just bear down, focus on the task and withdraw head down on the task **in their cave**, and some instead may need to express in words their feelings and yearn to be emotionally listened to. Solving the problem of many relationships often means just to understand how we cope differently with stress.

For example, women need to give their man some time in their cave. A man's cave is his antidote to stress. It's his meditation. It's his mindless relaxation – whatever he does in there. When a man says, "I'm ok," and retreats to his cave, women need to know that means, "I'm ok, I can deal with this by myself, I just need some time alone. I do not need any help. **Please support me by not worrying about me. Trust that I can deal with it all by myself.**" When men retrieve to their cave, it's not a good time to talk.

My friend Mike Foley makes a perfect example of this concept. We are both high-risk pregnancy physicians. When a birth defect has been detected in utero, some people withdraw and just start crying, needing to be held. Some start asking lots of questions, looking immediately to work hard at the best solution. Some express anger. Some fear. Some dismay. Some helplessness. These are **all normal human reactions**. The key is to understand that **being different is being normal**.

Modern life has thankfully made clear that **many men are Venusians, and many women are Martians**. And many are in between, with traits from both planets. It's so important to discover who we are. Gender orientation, the need to declare what we like, coming out as effeminate, or gay, or transsexual are helpful and wonderful first for ourselves, and then for those around us.

You should not feel guilty to end a relationship which you have realized has paired you with the wrong attachment style partner. Do not feel guilty for feeling incomplete or unsatisfied. The bottom issue is that your basic human individual needs are not met by this partner, and love alone isn't enough to make the relationship work.

In general, science has shown that **the more similar two people are, the fewer conflicts there will be**. And therefore the higher is the chance at a loving relationship. Similarity is most important in the biggest issues – for you - in life. These are often values as sincerity, honesty, trust. Spirituality and religion. Social interests. Including how much time to spend with friends, vs extended family (in-laws!). Social similarities might also include recreational activities such as sports, or opera.

Other important values are **goals in life** such as whether or not to have children and how many to have. Intellectual interests. As well as

vocational goals, e.g. how much committed to work we want to be and are willing to let our partner be. Being committed to the well-being of our partner is what love is all about. Having similar education, being able to communicate with each other on the same knowledgeable plane. It is good to have **intellectual** similarities.

These **commonalities lead to emotional unity**: feeling loved, respected, appreciated. To spiritual unity. To physical unity. And an ability to talk about old scars which might be creeping into this new relationship (e.g. "my ex-boyfriend was not committed to me, so I'll always be afraid you'd leave me"). It's best to be completely open, and keep no skeletons in the closet.

Commitment to core beliefs is key to long-lasting love. The core beliefs can be shared, or come mostly from one partner and be supported by the other.

This is the reason why science shows that **arranged marriages** often last a long time. Parents arrange a marriage with someone of similar culture, religion, location, social status, beliefs. Parents know their kids well, and hopefully try to match them also in terms of demeanor, likes, preferences, dreams. At times there is no initial passionate love, but empathic love can grow on the solid ground of many commonalities. I think arranged marriages should never happen, but I am making the point that similarities are helpful in a relationship.

There is a **cautionary tale about the facts that we are all a bit different**. You may be an anxious attachment type, who loves quality time and has learning as a major strength. You should be loved for what you are. But you should also not overdo it. Your main traits and strengths may get you in trouble if overused.

Your anxious style may be too much after a few hours of clinging to your partner. Your partner may need some space after a two-hour romantic walk just the two of you together. Your love of being on the computer to study the ancient Greeks' mythology does not mean that your partner has to be also interested in it, and you should expect that she might need to stop you after you have been 'flowing' on your computer for hours. We are all so very different.

Only when women and men and all of us are able to accept our differences, to understand that is normal and expected to be different, then love has a chance to blossom.

Discover what your essential love elements are

Perhaps for the world you're only someone, but for someone you are the whole world.

Gabriel García Márquez

Science has shown that there are at least 9 essential elements that form the basis on which long-term empathic love can flourish (Table 6). These are the basis of the pyramid of love (Figure 3).

Know who you are and what you like

Partners do not chose each other randomly. We mate with persons who already exist in our subconscious.

Sigmund Freud

It takes two to tango, as they say. We usually concentrate on what we would like in our partner. But the first most important step to be able to match well with our soul mate is to understand, truly, who we are. You need to be able to feel comfortable with yourself. You must know your strengths.[14] Your weaknesses. Your likings. Your wishes. Your dreams. Your plans for life. This is clearly the most important, basic step along the path to love happiness.

Being your authentic self contributes to your feeling of happiness and fulfillment. And being happy and fulfilled is one of the most attractive traits you can offer a partner. So for example if early on you discover that you desire closeness both emotionally and physically, and a potential partner wants instead to keep you at arm's length, you can end this relationship quickly and move on about finding someone who can fulfill your needs. And actually the unfit (for you) potential partner can discover how he can fit with someone else with different characteristics than yours.

Being confident in who you are will make you a more desirable partner. We should be aware of our strengths and virtues. There is a VIA classification of strengths and virtues which is helpful for all of us to be aware of. It includes shades of wisdom and knowledge, courage, humanity, justice, temperance, and transcendence (Table 8).[15]

Often **the love we get back from our partner is the mirror of what we feel about ourselves.** Some unfortunately feel worthless, and get treated as worthless. **Perhaps only at a certain age, once mature and comfortable with ourselves, with our strengths and weaknesses, we can truly aspire to have a good partner.** Some get to that age at 25. Many of us much later. Some unfortunately never.

Some have described **who we are in three ways.** One is the person perceived by others, by acquaintances and strangers. The middle one is the person perceived by our family and closest friends. The last is our true self, the one perhaps only we ourselves know.

In true love, we should strive to let our true self to be known to our lover. We should peel ourselves until the inner, truthful core. We need to be ourselves. Only the truth makes us free to be ourselves and to be loved for our factual self.

Love happiness is when what you think, what you say and what you do with yourself and your partner are in perfect harmony.

A related basic step is to **understand what characteristics are important for you in a love partner.** Many say they want someone who is beautiful, smart, wise, rich, who makes them laugh, tall, etc. It's hard to get all these features in one person. Instead **what we should do is concentrate on the main character traits most important for us.**

These are partner characteristics without which we just cannot love. That quality could be trust. Sincerity. Serenity. Passion. Courage. Pick just one or two initially, perhaps after looking at tables 6 and 7. And when you date, make sure the person has this trait, or traits. If they are blond or brunette, taller or shorter, in the long run that is less important.

I have learned for example that, **for me, positivity might be the most important trait.** I long for my partner's ability to look at life with a smile, to take good things well, but to also rejoice at a beautiful rainy day. It took me a lifetime to understand this. When I was 18, when asked what mattered to me in a love partner, I would have answered something like being 'tall and dark.'

That did not help me. In fact for example we know that fashion models are some of the unhappiest persons.[1] And that a beautiful unhappy person can bring you down. I really look for 'beauty inside' now, understanding that it would be nice to have beauty outside too, but inside beauty is just so much more important.

Another key part of knowing ourselves well is **understanding our childhood bliss as well as the wounds.** For me, I feel unconditionally loved by my mother, with physical touch and words of affirmation. My father was the opposite: he would only shake my hand, and praise me less than once a year, and never seemingly meaning it. It's important to accept who we are, what we faced, and what we need.

I longed to fix the relationship with my father by dating someone very similar to him: somebody who never praised, and disliked physical touch. I could not resolve it; a partner should not be changed to please our childhood struggles. What I really need is to have a partner like my mother, open, communicative, effusive in praise and physical touch. Thankfully I got exactly that with my wife, and there is bliss.

We must **avoid trying to fix our childhood wounds in our love relationship**. If we had little attention from a parent, we seek an avoidant partner trying to fix them to be loving and attentive to us every second of every day. This behavior is common, and a recipe for love disaster.

Our tendency to **select partners who share the negative traits of one of our parents** dooms the relationship from the start. If you did not get love as a child from an inattentive father, let's say, you are not going to get it now from an avoidant hypoaffective partner. One day you may realize that you are yearning for the behavior your partner can least give you.

Many people do not realize that they **keep fighting for a lifetime with their childhood demons, recreated with a partner who mirrors our parent's negative behavior**. I can see your mind going through your own relationships, and probably through many relationships of your friends, and realizing – I hope not too late!! – that so many have this pattern.

Another important part of discovering who you are in terms of what would make you achieve love happiness, is **trying yourselves in different relationships** before committing to one for the long-term. I loved a t-shirt I saw this year at Philadelphia Gay Pride: 'Fuck around until you find out.' It's direct, simple, clear.

You have to discover who you fit best with. On a physical level, and as or more importantly on an emotional level. There are so many different people out there. Interacting on a relationship level with some of them will help you to begin to come up with your preferred characteristics. Which should not be first physical, but more emotional, and related to attachment style, desire for intimacy, and types of love languages.

You might not know you like quality time until you date someone who does. You might not thing there are avoidant types out there until you date one. You might not think you like to dance until you try it with a partner who makes you feel wonderful while doing it.

Without knowing who you really are, what you like, and to be able to accept yourself and your preferences as worthy, there cannot be deep true love happiness.

Improve yourself where you can; accept the rest

An important part of getting to long-term love happiness is to **develop first ourselves a good character**. Establish good routine habits that are beneficial to yourselves, and your partner, and those around you. We should pick up in our lives good examples of behavior we admire. Initially often patterns from our parents, and then from those in the village around us. These pieces of the model eventually form a desirable self, ready to love and to be loved.

For example is so important to cultivate **gratitude**. Cicero said that gratitude not only is the greatest of virtues; it is also the parent of all others. Gratitude focuses the attention on what we already have. Gratitude celebrates the good in our life. Grateful people tend to be better at empathy and forgiveness, and more willing to help others. Being grateful makes us have greater life satisfaction, optimism, and prosocial behavior.

To become more grateful, just do The Three Good Things exercise. Evey evening write down three good things that happened that day, and why they happened. Gratitude focuses on the 'we,' not on the 'I.' It makes us appreciate what others, in our case specifically our partner, gave us, altruistically.

In fact at times The Three Good Things exercise should prompt us do a Grateful Visit.[16] We do something, like a note, an act of kindness, to show our gratitude to the person who was nice to us. Express openly your appreciation and gratitude to your partner. **Moments of reciprocal appreciation are like booster shots for romantic relationships**.

Be other-focused when expressing gratitude (this is not about you!). Be authentic, honest, sincere. And be context-sensitive: do not express gratitude by giving flowers if that is what you like and not what your partner likes.

And when you receive gratitude, accept it. Do not deflect it: "It was no big deal." That might sound dismissive. You also do not need to immediately reciprocate it. Accept it and cherish it. This is not a business transaction. By giving you sincere gratitude, your partner is acknowledging some goodness in you.

This is the best kind of love you can receive. Do not discount it. Somebody just thanked you for having done the grocery shopping. Do not return the kind words with some complain that there was not enough money to buy even more food. Do not insert negativity in a positive conversation.

Deflecting, reciprocating and discounting are ways of responding to our partner expression of gratitude without truly receiving it deeply and fully. Instead, we should try to accept, amplify, and advance the gratitude we receive. Accept gratitude by saying a heartfelt, "Thank you," while looking at the other person in the eye.

Amplify your gratitude by absorbing its rich qualities of love so to let it permeate your whole being. While receiving a back rub, purr, arch your back to demonstrate your pleasure, tell your partner how relaxed and loved you are feeling. Advance the gratitude and give feedback to say, "More here, less there, sure, great, continue please, should we try it on naked skin and some oil, etc," to give insight to our partner for ever greater connection next time.

Gratitude is like a dance, in which each partner has a role to play. Both initiation of the dance step, and response, must be carried out smoothly, positively. In fact, **a love relationship is also like a dance, an ongoing interaction of two people in which one initiates, the other follows, and then parts change again**, with the response person becoming for the next move the initiator, etc. The best couples have a good balance of initiation between the two partners.

As we dance, we are looking for attention, acknowledgement, affirmation, affection. We are looking for a partner who knows how to follow us at times, and to lead us at other times. We 'dance' with our partner so many times during the day, one person at a time making the request to 'dance.' We make bids for attention to our partner.

Research shows how we 'dance,' how we react to these bids, is very closely associated with how successful the couple will be at long-term love. Happy couples after many years in the relationship **respond positively to each other bids 84% of the time**.[17,18] The researcher Gottman could watch couples interact for a few minutes, and guess which one would stay together and which one would split a whopping 94% of the time.[17,18]

Kindness is another critical trait for cultivating positive empathic relationships. When happy long-term couples are asked about what they like about their partners, they most frequently praise their partner's kindness. **Kindness involves being positively oriented towards the other**. Kindness is motivated by emotional connection, a sense of common humanity with our partner, making us feel that they are worthy of our attention and care for their own sake.

Kindness is at the core of good positive relationships. Research shows that **happy long-term partners make five times as many positive comments as negative comments to each other**.[17] While you may not be a 'word of affirmation' or 'acts of kindness' kind of person, please remember these scientific data and how important it is to be kind to your partner.

Practicing kindness in fact can help you see yourself as more compassionate, therefore enhancing your self-perception. Wash the dishes. Empty the dishwasher. Do the laundry. Thank your partner. **Doing 5 acts of kindness a day on a single day each week enhances our own perceived level of happiness.**[19,20]

The way kindness is received is just as important as the way it is given. On the other side of this 'dance' of kindness, receiving kindness and love can help us move from egoism to altruism.

Another key to successful kindness is that **it has to be sincere**, and tactful towards the recipient. If our partner buys us gelato but we do not like gelato, the recipient should be grateful, but also point out that next time perhaps a salty delight may be even better appreciated.

A successful dance is based on awareness. You know what is happening to your body, what you like, and you learn what your partner likes along the dance. You learn your own and your partner's passions, emotions, preferences, strengths, weaknesses.

Focus on the uplifting moments, on the moments the dance is going so well you feel in flow, elated. Learn how to avoid stepping on each other's toes. Increase your awareness of what truly matters in your life. And nothing matters more than your relationship with your partner.

Look at the essential love elements (Table 6) and factors associated with long-term empathic love (Table 7) for improving your own persona, as you can, with the help of your partner. You should not pretend from your partner what you cannot do first yourself for her.

Your partner has to be open to love, and believe in love

Love is an act of faith, and whoever is of little faith is also of little love.
Erich Fromm

Love is **impossible if you or your partner are not open to love**. One needs to have a frame of mind suitable and compatible with empathic love. Some people are just happy by themselves. Research evidence shows that having someone next to us is helpful in being happy, but that person could be a mother, a sibling, a friend. A romantic partner has to be open to love in general as an essential factor for love happiness in a couple.

"**Amor, ch'al cor gentil ratto s'apprende ...**" Even Dante, almost 800 years ago, knew that love (amor) can occur only in a gentle heart (cor gentil), by which he meant a heart open to the possibility of love. We do not really make the other fall in love with us. **It's the other who is already predisposed to finding love, and lets himself fall in love.** In Dante's world, the propensity to love is a gentle trait.

Some have been 'burnt' by romantic love in the past, and are not open to suffer again. A good friend of mine was married for over two decades with her husband, who then told her he was gay and now lives with a male partner. That experience made her decide that she does not want the struggles of trying for love again; it's too much work for her.

Pain in past love relationships has made many people, LGBTQIA+, men, women, give up on romantic love, as they just do not have the will to try their luck again at something that has a chance of hurting them so deeply again. Please do not bother them, and do not fantasize you can change them. Look for another partner, not one who does not believe in being able to be in love happiness again.

My father wrote (in Italian) that, "**How one loves is the mirror revealing the character of the person.** Love does not mean to have, to possess, to be the owner; instead, it means to be owned. Love is not to use the other for our own gain; but to donate ourselves to our partner."

Not everyone is capable of this, or even believes in this altruistic love. Again, people without these beliefs will never make a good partner for you. We said love is wanting your partner's happiness; some people do not believe in this core principle. Please give up on the hope of a happy love relationship with such persons.

The one and only Sir Anthony Hopkins summarized this beautifully. *"**Let go of people who are not ready to love you.** This is the hardest thing you have to do in your life and it will be the most important. Stop having hard conversations with people who don't want to change. Stop showing up for people who don't care about your presence. I know your instinct is* *to do everything you can to gain appreciation for those around you, but it's an urge that steals your time, energy, mental and physical health.*

When you start fighting for a life of joy, interest and commitment, not everyone will be ready to follow you there. It doesn't mean you have to change who you are, it means you have to let go of people who aren't ready to join you. If you are offended, forgotten or ignored by the people you give your time to, you are not doing yourself a favor, by continuing to offer your energy and your life.

The truth is you are not for everyone and everyone is not for you. This is what makes it so special to find the people you have friendship with, or when love is reciprocated. The more time you spend trying to love someone who doesn't deserve it, the more time you waste depriving yourself of the possibility of that connection with someone else.

There are billions of people on this planet and many of them will meet you, at the level of interest and commitment you want. The more you engage with people who use you as a pillow, background choice, or therapist for their emotional therapy, the more you stay away from the community you want.

Maybe if you stop showing up, they won't look for you. Maybe if you stop trying, the relationship will end. Maybe if you stop texting, your phone will stay dark for weeks. That doesn't mean you ruined the relationship, it means the only thing you kept was the energy you gave just to keep it. This is not love, this is attachment. It is wanting to give a chance to those who don't deserve it!

You deserve a lot, there are people who should not be in your life, you will notice. The most valuable thing you have in your life is your time and energy as both are limited. What you put in time and energy will determine your existence. When you realize this, you begin to understand why you are so anxious when you spend time with people, activities, places or situations that don't suit you and shouldn't be around you, they steal your energy.

Make your life a safe haven where only "compatible" people are allowed with you. You are not responsible for saving anyone. You are not responsible to convince them to improve. It's not your job to exist for people and give your life to them!

Your only obligation is to realize that you are the master of your destiny and to accept the love you think you deserve. Decide that you deserve a true friendship, a true commitment and a complete love with healthy and prosperous people. Then wait and see how much everything will start to change and, that's for sure, positive and good energy people will come.

Don't waste your time on people who don't deserve it. *Change will give you love, appreciation, happiness and protection in the position you deserve."*

I myself followed this advice several times. Sometimes after making initially unwise choices. I spent over a year together with a girl who told me the first night we met she had attempted suicide after her prior relationship. She would remain in a bad mood even during a vacation in Florida. My frame of mind was often, "...**but I can change her**. I, I!!, can make her happy eventually." I never did make her happy. She was just not a happy person, at least when paired with me.

Women make this misjudgment often. They fall in love with a depressed, pessimistic soul. Or a lazy boy. Or a criminal. Or a violent bully. They think, "Oh, I can change him." But that's an illusion. The difficult past of that guy is often too deep and ingrained in his being; he cannot change.

Men do this with some women, too. People who have problems are not always looking to get fixed. They actually want to take the partner into their world, be it laziness, criminality, violence, or other. Do not tolerate yelling. Do not let anyone humiliate you.

Please get out of your relationship if you have realized you could not make your partner happy. You cannot love someone who does not want her own happiness; it's against the definition of love, which is 'striving to make your partner happy.' You cannot love her; and you will never feel loved.

In these situations, your partner likes being unhappy. She wants others to feel unhappy with her. She disliked it when you are happy – which for me for example is pretty much constantly. You feel your partner is more content when she can bring you down into her problems, her complaints, her negativity. She does not want to be 'perked up.' She likes it when she can actually express her negativity of people, of events, for quite some time. Many people are like that.

In friendship, I've learned to practice the same principle. **I stopped calling friends who did not call me**, at least once in a while. And I do appreciate a wife who is happy to be loved by me. And those true friends who do call me. Those who do want to spend quality time with me.

Love demands both sides being open hearted. There must be **predisposition on both sides** to make ample space for the relationship. The two beings are open to bearing each other's soul to the other. If one person is content of his status quo, he is probably not ready for the revolution that falling in love brings. He does not feel the necessity to break with the past.

The person open to romantic love knows there is something missing in her life. She is ready for something new. She is already looking for something. She is, openly or unconsciously, almost ashamed of not having someone to love, someone who loves her. That is why falling in love happens often during momentous life changes.

Adolescence is when falling in love comes easiest. It is a natural way to be at this stage of life. We are changing to a new person, a new being capable of loving. Falling in love at times happens to us as adults when our kids go to college, and we have to face the reality of a relationship which does not give us what we want. So we look elsewhere for love happiness.

In fact, common misconception is that passionate love belongs just to the young. If an adult falls in love, **she is called an immature**. She is called 'a baby.' She is called unserious. Institutions hate change. Old people despise the peril of seeing someone risk it all, unless they are young with nothing to lose. Society often derides the single adult still looking for 'my other half.'

My heroes are indeed people who believe in love all the way to the end of life. Falling in love is a lottery with not always a great chance of winning. **Those who already have money in the bank – a love tank not empty – do not play the lottery. Love is risky**, no question about it. Many people out there are risk-averse. Thankfully, some people are willing to work hard to truly live, instead of merely surviving.

Predisposition to new love **flourishes in those who somehow do not feel loved, and long for love**. Those who still see some happy couples, some successful marriages. Those who feel they want to become the half of a future happy couple. Those who want to feel the intensity of passion, and do not want to feel excluded from joy.

Many people in unhappy relationships instead keep on trying to enjoy the challenges. The difficulties. The more problematic, the more negative, the more we want to play 'good Samaritan,' and try to change our partner. But most times, our partner does not want to change. They are quite fine with their pessimism, depression, negativity. Or they are just 'not that much into us.'

They could care less if we are happy or not, really. They have no idea our happiness depends on theirs. In fact, they rather bring us down to their pessimism, than to rise to our optimism. They even tell us this to our face. But we often we do not believe them.

I am telling you now loud and clear: believe in what the partner says, and does. Do not live in lalaland. Do not dream a fairytale which has no chance of becoming reality. Love should be based on the facts. Love needs to be based on reality.

'He is not that much into you' is a great movie to understand that sometimes, the other side just does not corresponds the same deep feelings you have. When I watched this movie, I had a 'aha' moment. Try to watch this movie when you are 20-25 years old, not when you are 70 and a bit later in the pursuit of love happiness.

Oriana Fallaci, one of my favorite Italian writers, said that *"unilateral love is not enough. One should not gift her soul to someone else unwilling to gift love back. Who does not give gifts, does not appreciate gifts. One can desperately look for love, and donate all herself in love. But the partner's love cannot just be wished; hoped for; must be there, must exist on its own. Love is a dialogue, not a monologue."*

Some get hurt so much by a broken love story that they give up. For the rest of their lives. As Alberto Alberoni said in *Innamoramento e amore*, they become petrified. **They become like stones, unwilling to change, unwilling to let someone else ever again in their lives, in their souls. The pain of a crushed love has been too much**.

Both partners must believe in love. Love is an act of faith, of great courage. When you stop believing in your relationship, or your partner does, nothing will bring it back. Many stop believing not only on their failing current relationship, but sadly in all possible future relationships, and give up on romantic love.

Often it is women who stop believing in a relationship. And stop believing in love. And when they do, they do not change their mind. Their trust in the partner is gone. **Their trust in finding love is gone.** So give up on the woman who left you. Do not delude yourself that she really still loves you; that she'll change her mind; that she'll come back; she won't.

A good friend of mine stays with his wife of over 30 years so to have her make him some tea in old age, to have somebody to go to the movies on Saturday evening, and to avoid loneliness. Love involves all that, and should also be more than that.

Therefore, to give true love a chance, both partners should from the beginning be caring, open to failure, open to getting hurt, determined, courageous, honest by speaking by facts, energetic, good listeners, coherent in what she and he do and what she and he say. Some of us, but not all of us, have an **irresistible need to love.**

A related corollary to the 'love belief' is the **willingness to commit**. For example, at some point, the issue of **living together**, and even to marry or somehow make the relationship 'official' for example by buying a house together, will present.

I am for living together once the bond is strong enough, and there is hope in each partner for a long-term relationship. Living together allows us to discover even more about our partner, such as interest in cooking, cleaning, other household issues, sleeping patterns, etc. It pays to discover if there are traits that we just cannot live with long term.

Moreover, willingness to commit enough to let the world know you are a couple, is a paramount step at some point. Secrecy and unwillingness to commit means one of the partners is not committed.

Your partner has to love you

The thing is, I'm just a girl, standing in front of a boy, asking him to love her.

Julia Roberts, in Notting Hill

Your partner should **wiggle his tail** when he is with you. He has to cuddle; he has to want your happiness, the way *you* like to be happy; he has to be able to give you what you want the most. He should not be with you just for money, convenience, because his parents would be happy. **Choose someone who wiggles her tail when she sees you.**

William Somerset Maugham said that, "The love that lasts longest is the love which is never returned." It may be true, but it is so sad. I accept it when someone 'loves' a cat; wants the happiness of the cat, hoping nothing in return. **I believe instead that when one loves a human being, being loved back is the ultimate love happiness. It's the completion of the circle.**

When one recognizes and appreciates the partner's strengths, he is more likely to be happy in his relationship, to have his own needs met, and to be more sexually satisfied.[20] If you see that your partner does not admire you, worship you, appreciate you, then you are probably not with the right partner.

You should first love yourself, and then have next to you a partner who loves you and treats you well. Otherwise you'll get used to being mistreated, and eventually you won't love yourself either. Love requires you to make a major investment and effort. You need fertile ground to make sure your own effort falls on ears and mind and body who appreciate it. I have talked with so many who feel like their love efforts were not properly matched by their partner. This is very sad, and we should put remedy to this.

The movie, **"She is not that much into you"** is a revelation for many people, not just me. Looking back, I met many nice girls who were not into me. They might have liked me some. But **they were not in love.** They never thought I was truly what they were looking for themselves in terms of romantic love.

Sure, perhaps they thought I was smart. Some perhaps thought I was a good guy. But they did not think, feel that I was the one they truly thought they would want to make happy, i.e. want to love. I appreciate those who told me right away that they were not into me, so that a romantic relationship never started, and I suffered much less.

We must all realize we won't be liked by all, and certainly not be loved by all. But many refuse to look at the reality of rejection. "**She is afraid to love me**," we tell ourselves, and tell even our confidantes. "She would love to date me, but cannot not because...," with some lame excuse. We even invent the most spectacular of non-sensical excuses for not being loved back, "**She does love me, but she does not know it.**"

The list of excuses of the not-in-love partner is long as well. "**I love you, but currently I do not feel ready for a relationship.**" This means usually, "I am actually ready for a relationship, but not with you. I think actually I'd like someone who does not cling on to me so much, as you do. I'd prefer someone to conquer perhaps, someone who does not love me and that I have to pain for."

Or, "I'm still blocked from the memories of my past story," i.e. "I do not like you enough to make me forget my last love experience." Or, "I'm afraid to tie myself too tightly to you," i.e. "I do not want to tie myself into you."

Or, "I'm afraid to make you suffer," i.e. "I'm afraid to be suffocated by your attentions, even if I'll need once in a while to be in touch and make you suffer, at least until I do find my true love, which is not you."

Other examples are, "I do not deserve you," i.e. "I do not love you enough to bear a relationship as serious as you want it." Or, "We are too similar," i.e. "You are so boring."

So **cut off relationships in which you do not truly love the other. And those in which you are not loved.** You cannot fix these by talking, even by chatting your head off. The right time is now. You have waited enough. Do not keep on living in illusions. Do not fool yourself: your love, or their love, is not enough. Only accept both together. **Use your energy not to change someone's mind about you. Use your energy to meet someone who needs no convincing.**

We must avoid living in our dream of a relationship. We want a warm, sensual, cuddly, trustful partner; so the next girl we meet, we immediately tell ourselves unconsciously, or even consciously, that she has all the traits we want. She does not have them, unless proven wrong after months of close encounters. We cannot love just our idea of a partner; we must know our partner well first, and understand at least if she meets our unnegotiable basic requirements.

I think many issues can be fixed in a love relationship. We can and should compromise on many fronts. But we cannot fix not being loved. We should not accept not being loved back. **We cannot remedy feeling unloved**.

It **takes courage to stop a relationship** in which our love is not reciprocated. It is indeed a clear acceptance on our part that we have failed. That despite having shown our best self, despite having tried to love the other the way she wants to be loved, we have failed in getting her love reciprocated to us.

To tell the truth, I am proud I did have the courage to end relationships who did not have reciprocal love in them. From me to my partner. Or from my partner to me, which was obviously much more painful. Some said I would never have the courage to admit defeat. Well, **I lost, and admitted defeat. You can only win long-term by accepting to lose at times**. And I've always kept the faith that love for me existed.

Accepting defeat in love in fact reveals great maturity, great strength of character. One should not change oneself to accept non-love. One cannot change the other and by miracle make them love us, if we can see and feel that they do not love us. **Love cannot, and should not, be forced**. So it's important to have the lucidity to stop relationships in which love is lacking from one side. And sometimes even lacking from both sides.

Accepting defeat made me a better person. Made me an honest person in front of the world. Made me understand what I wanted. Made me peaceful and happy inside, especially once I found what I really was yearning for. I think accepting defeat made me an example for others, my kids in particular, not to give up. Especially not to give up on love, the most important thing.

Accepting defeat in a game which you cannot win, is smart and liberating. Like quitting a job we do not like, a job we do not find fulfilling and goal-oriented. By quitting a bad game, we can get to play a new better game. We can play a game which caters to our strengths. It's like if we are good at soccer, but we are asked to play a baseball game. Or vice versa. Play the game you are best at, with the best teammate.

I cannot stand staying together only so that when we are old, someone will be a faithful roommate. Love is that, but a lot more than that. **Your partner has to make you feel good, happy.** You can feel it in your heart when you have a true life partner. You should face your feelings when they tell that, despite your best labors, you do not feel reciprocated in love.

A corollary to these concepts is that fact that **the love partner should be the most important person for the other partner.** No ifs, ends or butts. The chosen love partner should hold a higher stature in our heart and soul than our kids, mother, father, brother, sister, grandmother, grandfather, best friend.

In the past, when I was much younger, I had trouble 'giving up' putting my mother down from her #1 spot. I was wrong, and this compromised a bit some early relationships. I then learned my lesson, and now I'm all in putting, in any issue in life, my wife as my #1 focus, love, person. Do not accept anything less from your romantic partner.

Courage

Love is everything is cracked up to be. It's really worth fighting for, being brave for, risking everything for. And the trouble is, if you don't risk anything, your risk is even greater.
Erica Young

We are never so vulnerable as when we love.
Sigmund Freud

Love requires courage. The courage to not just stare at the sea. But to dress down to the bathing suit, almost naked, and jump in. Even if we know the water might be cold; and rough. And so we might get hurt.

Some devote their whole lives to avoiding risks. They will not be able to find love happiness. Rather than enlarging themselves, they narrow and diminish their lives to just mere survival. A full life has risks, and joys. The attempt to avoid challenges and potential suffering is at the core of much mental disease.

So love requires openness to the next encounter. One should not take all the negativity from prior experiences to the next relationship. Just because the prior partner cheated on us, it does not mean the next one will. We cannot obsesses her with our fears. We need to stay open, stay positive, we need to smile and think forward, not backward. Stay mind light, not mind locked and heavy and closed.

Albert Einstein said, *"I must love someone. Otherwise it is a miserable experience. And that someone is you."* I agree with him. I feel the same way. I feel wasted without being able to love someone. I have love talents inside me to give others. And I think they are good deeds, good capacities. Not everyone wants to give love; not everyone wants to receive love. Do not chose such people as the aim of your romantic love.

Altruism

Give love and kindness to others, expecting nothing in return.
Elisa Medhus

One of the deep secrets of life is that all that is really worth doing is what we do for others.
Lewis Carroll

Living for others it's not only our rigorous duty, but also it is our path to happiness.
August Compte

Do unto others as you would have them do unto you. Treat others as you would like to be treated. Practically every religion has this as the golden rule for human interaction. In quite a number of areas, our partners do not want what we want; that's normal. **Altruism is perhaps the most important key to love happiness. Stop giving to your partner what you want; give her what she wants.**

Treat others as they wish to be treated. And, even better, **treat the other person as her best self would want us to treat her**. Help their inner good grow and develop. As you nurture them, altruistically making them feel loved and appreciated, your reciprocal attraction and esteem will grow. We are attracted to our partners by the good we see in them. So seeing them be good people motivates us to become better people ourselves.

Love cannot even start without altruism. **Love starts when one person is willing to gift himself into another person**, wishing not only his own happiness, but more importantly that of the other. The only benefit the person who takes the initiative to love has, is the hope of long-term empathic love happiness, in which both partners donate each other to the other.

Studies have shown that **motivation to care for the welfare of another being, or communal motivation** as psychology calls it, is linked to greater relationship well-being for both members of the relationship.[21]

Love is giving to others. Unwillingness to share the housework is one of the main causes of divorce and the end of love relationships. **Inequality is inadmissible in our modern world.** There should be no power struggle over who does the housework. If it's the only solution, get house chores help please, before fighting over who does the laundry.

If you are selfish, you cannot love. A love relationship cannot involve keeping score, like in a game; the moment one starts keeping score, he has lost.

To reach love happiness, we need to be **able to give love away with oblivious abandon without calculating the chances of it ever being returned**. We act as givers, not as matchers or as takers.[22] **You can only**

commit to mature love when you are ready to love someone, not just when you want to be loved.

It's **like the love we give to a child**. We love an imperfect being and want her to be happy and to develop into whatever person she is meant to be herself. We are there as constant support, forgiving mistakes, finding strengths to cultivate, providing emotional and physical help.

Part of being altruistic is to **purposely perform caring acts of kindness to our partner**. Push your partner to write down some loving behavior they would love to receive. Classic examples are spending more quality time together talking, getting a foot massage, an evening out for dinner. And then purposely perform on a routine basis these acts of love.

Through daily repetition of positive behaviors, the receiving partner begins again to perceive the giving partner as someone 'who nurtures me.' The 'tit for tat' issue must be avoided. There is no reason to feel good about a pleasant act received if there is on it a price tag to repay the pleasantness later with something we hate to do.

The 'quid pro quo' – *latin* literally for 'this for that' – should be banned. A favor is done altruistically with no hope for return. We should be givers in love, not matchers, or, even worse, takers. The back rub must come and be perceived as a gift, with no strings attached.

This goes back again to our childhood psyche, when we expected pleasantries and gifts from our parents, expecting not to have to reciprocate the kind acts. In adulthood, we still crave to receive this altruistic love. And of course we must be able to give love altruistically too, as a mature loving adult.

Do to others what you would want them to do to you. That is why I do like some aspects of ancient religions. This principle is eternal, and a 'sine-qua-non' (an essential condition, from the *latin*, 'without which, no') of empathic love. If your partner craves having coffee made in the morning, prepare things in the evening so that coffee is ready and easily available when your partner wakes up.

Repetitive acts of kindness are priceless. Moreover, **random acts of loving kindness** reinvigorate the routine. Surprise pleasantries are wonderful. While repetitive acts may be expected after a while, **an unpredicted kindness rekindles the feeling of being loved**.

Being altruistic in a love relationship means also to want the partner to achieve their life goals, to understand what they were born to do and how best they can contribute to a better world. **Discovering the strength of one's partner and helping her master those strengths** will make for a happier, more satisfied partner, and therefore a better love relationship.

When one truly loves, one wishes to do things for the other. One wishes to sacrifice. One wishes to serve.

Positivity

Some cause happiness wherever they go; other whenever they go.
                                    Oscar Wilde

Good humor is goodness and wisdom combined.

Choose as a love partner someone who is already happy inside. Happy relationships have been shown by research to have positivity of each partner towards each other, supersede the moments of negativity. Their positivity causes them to feel optimistic about one another and their relationship, to have positive expectations about their lives together, and to give each other a pass when an issue seems to come up.

It's like positivity helps the couple raise a high bar, so that it would take a lot more negativity to bring it down, than if the set point were lower. **The person we love empathically conserves the characteristics of our ideal love**, and we forgive his faults.

Partners in these positive relationships assume the best about each other and their relationship. They are able to understand and acknowledge each other's perspective, at least to some extent, even when they disagree. They respect the other's point of view, as they admire their partner as a human being.

They are attuned to each other's emotions. They might not be similar, but there is deep understanding that reactions are ok since the person is ok. There is sympathy versus one another, a **willingness to accept a different way of interpreting the same issue**. There is no hard

90

stand against another's argument without first deeply understanding where that unexpected view comes from.

Love lasts when we focus on the positives. This is similar to what happens to our love for our father, mother, siblings. We become aware over time of their faults. Their shortcomings. But we can try to rationalize things for the good. Dad is nervous and mean at times; perhaps it's because he works so much. Mom is not as warm as I'd like; she was raised by cold parents.

The best way to deal with our emotions is to share them. Not to hide them. Fear is the most powerful of emotions. **Positive emotions turn on our curiosity and desire to engage and explore. They set us up for openness and learning**. Joy invigorates us. Watching a joyful video clip, for example, make our brain work better on the next task.

Choose the dog who is wagging their tail when you meet them, and then in general when you are together. A friend of mine has been married for over 30 years to someone who, when they first met, told her as first words, "Fuck off." That is not a good start.

We should do our part as well. **Never stop smiling, even if you're down, because you never know who might fall in love with your smile**, as Gabriel García Márquez said. **Be a 'yes' person; not a 'no' first person**. Like people from the start; give them a chance; do not fear that everyone out there is out to get you. I love a positive, can do, hopeful and realistic attitude.

The best is having someone next to you who is happy. If you cannot make the person next to you happy, that is failure. At least for me, but truly for the great majority of us. I want to make everyone happy. If I cannot make the person next to me happy, I have failed.

The issue is, **some people are just not happy themselves**. And so it's hard, or impossible really, for you to make them happy, which is not in their genes. People who try to change the partner's basic demeanor usually fail. You cannot change their DNA. About 50% of happiness is genetically determined.[1] And cannot be changed. **Get tired quickly of a negative person**.

While men unfortunately err into seeking a woman in particular based on looks, women often look for men who have broad shoulders.

This is a stereotype, but also confirmed by studies. We should all instead focus on people who have a positive attitude. Thankfully, often the 'broad shoulders' women seek in a man, are as much physique as attitude and character.

We should focus on characteristics as in table 6. **And accept positively the other person for who she is.**

Positive psychology is the science that focuses on human strengths and potentials and celebrates what's best in life. It was launched in 1998 at the University of Pennsylvania here in Philadelphia by Martin Seligman. It emphasizes goals, well-being, satisfaction, happiness, interpersonal skills, perseverance, talent, wisdom, and personal responsibility.

Positive psychology highlights that **happiness is largely a result of how we choose to respond to what happens to us.** It teaches us to look at the glass half full, and be grateful for what we have, and to change away from pessimism. Positive Psychology is the contrary of being depressed.

While for centuries medicine and psychology have focused on curing the person with depressed mood, positive psychology aims to prevent us from getting depressed in the first place, by focusing on the positive things we already have, and aiming to get ourselves more things that make us happy, actively.

Perhaps the most important lesson that positive psychology teaches us, is that **other people matter for our happiness, and the one who matters the most is our partner**. Having someone with a positive outlook on life who also loves us altruistically can make a good life great.

The **top ten list of positive emotions**, according to research by Fredrickson,[23] are:

- Joy
  - Brightness in demeanor, e.g. birth of your child
- Gratitude
  - Appreciation for what you have, e.g. the feeling after a friend did you a huge favor you really cared about
- Serenity

- o Laid-back safety and comfort, e.g. sitting on the beach and listening to the sounds of the waves
- Interest
  - o A desire to learn more, e.g. you want to learn how to sail
- Hope
  - o We see the future in a positive way, things will improve, e.g. a bad diagnosis is temporary, and treatment will cure it
- Pride
  - o You feel good about something you did, e.g. the garden you worked hard on is in beautiful full bloom
- Amusement
  - o Shared laughter, e.g. you share an hilarious joke
- Inspiration
  - o Uplift we feel when we see human excellence, e.g. hearing our partner has helped a struggling student despite being so busy herself with the rest of her classrooms
- Awe
  - o Witnessing extreme level of goodness, so a notch above inspiration, e.g. our partner did something so good that we feel overwhelmed by greatness and suspended momentarily in time
- Love
  - o When all the above feelings stir our heart within a safe, close relationship, we call it love. Interest in the person moves to amusement, and then joy. We share our hopes with the loved one, and that leads to serenity. Feelings of gratitude and pride develop. Inspired by our partner's qualities and good character, we experience awe. Each of these moments leads to the positive emotion of love.

Positive emotions broader our attention, increase the range of possible thoughts we might have, and increase the type of actions we might take in a particular context, making us more prone to be proactive and improve whatever discussion or situation we are in.

Even just watching a video clip with a positive message, changes our brain to have a broader view of thinking. Positive emotions turn on our curiosity and desire to engage and explore. They set us up for openness and learning, and invigorate us.

Positive emotions make us more creative, so we are **able to solve complex problems better and quicker.** Research shows that physicians in a positive mood make better diagnoses compared to their less-positive colleagues.[24]

When we are feeling joyful, we are 'feeling up.' Our eyes are looking up and around, our shoulders are straight, we are breathing slowly and deeply, and our minds are active and lively. Positive emotions open us up, making us more receptive and more creative. When we feel joy, we want to play and be creative. We want to explore and to learn new things. We want to savor our experience and integrate it into a new view of ourselves and the world.

Research shows that when we experience positive emotions we enjoy lower levels of stress-related hormones, and higher levels of beneficial hormones. So that our blood pressure is lower, we have less pain, fewer colds, better sleep.

With positive emotions we also benefit from a lower likelihood of hypertension, diabetes, and stroke, and are more likely to live longer. Psychologically we are more optimistic, more resilient, more open, more accepting, and more driven by purpose.

Prioritize positivity in yourself, in your partner, in your relationship. Make decisions and organize your life in ways that are most likely to result in the experience of positive emotions. Sign up for an exercise class together; complete do-it-yourself projects at home; go out to dinner together once a week; take a little trip together. Watch the sunset, listen to music together. Go dancing. A happy partner should be contagious in a mature long-term love relationship.

Trust

If love persists, it means there's friendship. What's friendship? It's intimacy, it's telling each other everything. It's total trust in the other, it's telling to oneself: "This one is not going to cheat me."
                                    Johann Wolfgang von Goethe

Success moves at the speed of trust.

Trust is one of the main factors over which love can live and prosper (Figure 3). Trust is for love happiness what food, water, heat and shelter are for our survival in general.

Trust leads to safety and security. Being in a successful intimate love relationship should feel like what we felt when as infants we were being protected by the arms of a parent. It's the same feeling of safety and security. It's the unconditional love our parents gave us: we can feel our partner is going to love us as we are, including our flaws. Our partner now helps us in our struggle to survive all outside struggles.

We have to be able to trust our partner. In a sense, the weaker ones try to control the partner, instead of trusting her. Too much control over the partner inhibits both our emotions, and of course those of our partner. Trust enables intimacy, openness, the full sharing of emotions.

Being **emotionally attuned to our partner** is another important element of trust. John Gottman, in his book 'The Science of trust,'[24] outlines that key elements are attention, turning toward, tolerance, understanding, non-defensive responding, and empathy.

We need to be trusting in a partner who is **not only loyal to us physically, but also emotionally attuned to what we are feeling or what we might need**. Loyalty of the heart is more vital than physical loyalty, but both are super-important.

The last central concept I want to emphasize regarding trust is **self-trust when one is in love**. It's the feeling, often unconscious, that there is no other person who could be our love partner, as we are way too in love with our current partner. We feel so good being with our current partner that we do not see, dream, fantasticate on anyone else. Even advances from a suitor do not surface to our awareness.

While trust is a must, it does not come easy. Doubt, suspicion, blatant cheating, physical or emotional, is all around us, and around the corner. Unfortunately often adults, not only youths, want to relive passionate love and see it as more possible with a different person than with their long-term partner. The thrill of stage 1 joyful romance, being displayed by media all around us every day of our lives, is seemingly irresistible.

One needs instead to stay rational. We have chosen to stay in our relationship for important, basic qualities we found in our partner. **Seeking a new thrill means betraying the trust of our current lover, and therefore destroying everything we have built with him**. The mental intimacy, the shared values, not just the house and kids. The loss is often overwhelming and can lead to depression and suicide. **We get blinded by what we gain with the affair, without realizing what we lose in what is already in front of us**.

This book is all about being courageous, and finding true long-lasting love. It is for ending relationships which we have tried to improve for years and with professional help but make us empty and unhappy. But **it's important to avoid tipping the scale with the goal of getting out as a way of escaping the hard work of a positive love happy partnership**. In fact, as a constructive relationship can get a bit boring by being so good and stable, the thrill for an escape into the wild may occur even more than in unstable and troubled relationships.

Respect

Respect is another important pillar of long-term empathic love (Figure 3). **Respect is wanting the best for our partner because we believe our partner deserves it**. It is not cheating because we are aware there is no better partner for us. Because we feel truly loved by our partner, and cannot live any more without that love. We love because we respect our partner's way of life, her sacrifices for us, the gratitude we feel towards her.

The emotionally intelligent partner is able to understand and honor the wishes of the partner. He answers, "Yes, and …," and not "Yes, but …" He is aligned with his lover's wants.

People should not perceive their partner to be inferior. They should not perceive their partner to be superior. **Partners should perceive each other as equals.** That is when the relationship can avoid most conflict and be stable.

Partners need to **treat each other well. We should continuously try to charm our partner. I love the idea of being more polite, more well dressed, more respectful, more open to communication and more altruistic at home than outside the home.** More empathic at home than outside the home. We should be putting always our partner first, above everyone else, above all else. We can't let our partner think the dog is more important in our life than them.

One of the most important issues to appreciate as a partner in a love relationship is that **it's crucial to understand the truth of the other person.** You have to believe in your heart that your partner is as real as you, as right as you, and her feelings matter as much as yours.

One must acknowledge that, when in a partnership, **your own feelings aren't the end of the story. There are many realities: here is mine, here is yours, equally real, equally important.** We should push ourselves to enter our partner's world. We might not like to watch golf, but our partner is so happy when we sit next to him watching it on tv, even for just a few minutes.

We might not enjoy shopping, but our partner is delighted when we do, together. This all starts with **respect for each other's likings, wishes, routines, dreams.** We should not only respect them as reasonable, but learn over time to **consider them a magical way to come closer in love.**

Forget a physical identikit

Many a man has fallen in love with a girl in light so dim he would not have chosen a suit by it.
$\hspace{3cm}$ *Gabriel García Márquez*

There is only one kind of love, but there are a thousand imitations.
$\hspace{3cm}$ *François de La Rochefoucauld*

Each of us has in our heart an identikit of the person we want as lover. That image is a mix of characteristics we have learned from our parents in particular, but also from school, friends, other adults, and our prior love experiences. When we fall in love, often the person has some or many of the characteristics we thought absolutely necessary for us, as he fits almost to the 't' our identikit. We go, "Here he is."

Given society's continuous bombardment towards esthetical appearance, **our ideal identikit for a love partner is often full of physical traits. When I was 18, mine was tall, thin, brunette, dark big eyes**. It had some characteristics of my mother, and the focus my father told me about: "Make sure you are happy in 20 years with how she looks in bed. You do not want to turn around and see a witch."

For decades, I followed the wrong description of who I wanted. It is so much better to have a 'values' identikit. The values described in Tables 6 and 7. Think about how musicians and singers are often (or at least should be) chosen: best if being a curtain – when looks do not influence the music they are able to magically express with their instrument.

This has been reported in many studies, and surveys. For example, a match.com survey revealed that 94% of daters want someone they can **trust and confide in**; 92% of daters want someone who **is comfortable communicating their wants and needs**; 92% of daters want someone who is **emotionally mature**; 92% of daters want someone who can **make them laugh**; 89% of daters want someone who is **comfortable with their own sexuality**.[25] People are beginning to understand what counts.

Your love partner should be chosen first based on whatever values (not looks) you think most important. If models are the most unhappy persons in the planet, why chose on looks? You have to like her with your heart and mind, not just with your eyes. Some of this is actually unconscious. Sometimes, if we are truly focused on values instead of on looks, we end up attracted to people we did not think we would like.

An amazing example of these issues is the story of **Marilyn Monroe**. Marilyn is even today one of the most admired, wanted women who ever existed. She is on all the list of the most beautiful, most desired, sexiest women who ever lived. She died at 36 after probably committing suicide, or at least taking so many anxiety and anti-depressant pills as to overdose on them.

Looks did not make her happy. She got married 3 times in her young life, and still never found love happiness. In fact she committed suicide as she had felt used by both Bob and Jack Kennedy, who were both recent lovers of hers.

Perhaps the most revealing and sad part about Marilyn's love life is that her mother conceived her with a lover while married to someone else, and Marilyn did not get to know the identity of her father until an adult. Her mother was quite unstable, had mental disorders, and so Marilyn was raised first by other relatives, and eventually in 12 foster homes.

She was sexually abused as a 12 year old. She found escape by marrying at 16 years of age. She had grown up unable to trust adults, without the unconditional love so necessary for a normal development, and with the feeling of being a sex object unable to obtain true love.

Joe DiMaggio and Arthur Miller, her second and third husbands, were probably good men truly in love with her. But they were unable to grow long-term empathic love with her given her anxious, may be even avoidant attachment style. Marilyn probably did not believe in love as she had not experienced it while young.

In fact she suffered mostly neglect and abuse growing up, which she unconsciously perpetrated as an adult, reliving her youth full of abusive powerful men which would take advantage of her. It is so sad to say, but trying to grow long-term empathic love with someone like Marilyn Monroe is very, very difficult, and at times truly impossible.

It's important to also understand what love is not. Love is not economic security. Love is not feeling important next to a physically attractive person. Love is not having someone in the same house to feel secure at night. Love is not being with someone because others admire her.

Love is not having someone to avoid loneliness or boredom. Love is not being with a powerful person to feel admired and pampered. Love is not just great sex. Love is not being with someone to piss someone else off. Love is not just having a travel companion.

The beauty of long-term empathic love is that it transcends initially, and later, physical beauty. If your soul mate happens to be beautiful when you go through passionate love, **the loss of beauty, the wrinkles, the double chin, the gray hair, the loss of hair will not be noticed and won't interfere with long-term empathic love flourishing on much more important value**s (Tables 6 and 7).

Sexual intimacy

A kiss: a silent promise.

A romantic relationship involves **sexual intimacy** - a friendship does not. If you are married to someone and you have no sexual intimacy, you are in a friendship, not a romantic relationship, and that is something you will need to decide if you want to change.

Plato, in Symposium, described **the myth of Aristophanes**, concerning the origin of sexual love. The original inhabitants of Earth were round creatures with 4 hands and 4 feet and with their backs and sides forming a circle. These self-sufficient sexless beings were very arrogant and repeatedly attacked the gods. To punish them, Zeus hurled thunderbolts at them and split them apart. Each creature was now two, each half longing to merge with its other half.

Interestingly, Aristophanes said that **originally there were 3 genders**. So there were males, females, and androgynous humans with characteristics of both male and female. **If the androgynous human was** split in two, the two half – one male and one female – would be looking for each other the rest of their lives, like in heterosexual love.

If a male was split in two, two guys would look for each other, like in gay men attracted to men. And if a female was split in two, two lesbians would be looking for each other the rest of their lives.

The brain is the most erogenous organ. Women imagine broad shoulder that can defend them, and a strong partner with whom to be able to protect her and the kids. Men imagine the wide hips of their partners will bear healthy kids, and the red lips will give luscious kisses.

Sexual arousal **starts with what we imagine. Vaginal lubrication and penile erection start even before a physical touch**, a kiss, a hug, a caress. A glance, a softness in her voice, an accomplice smirk in his face, are more than enough to spark sexual attraction and open the gates to a flood of hormonal changes.

Sexual intimacy is not just intercourse. A simple relationship **kiss** is a powerful thing. **Kisses are very intimate, especially kisses on the mouth.** Remember Vivian's rule in Pretty Woman? She'd do just about anything as a prostitute, but no kissing on the mouth. Kissing on the mouth was just too intimate.

It is also crucial to make sure that when you do connect, it's with a '**good kiss.**' No matter how busy your life is, the time it takes to be in the moment for a kiss with your partner will not derail your schedule.

Kiss each other when you say goodbye in the morning, when you come home at night, when you go to bed, when you're leaving on a trip. Surprise each other with kisses on the fly. Even give a sleeping spouse a kiss when you leave or come home at odd hours.

Every time you kiss, you show the other person how special he or she is to you. Kissing will also help reaffirm your attachment to them. Too often, people tell me that they feel like they're just friends with their spouse. They say that there is no longer any touching and a lack of kissing in a relationship. They talk about being really great roommates.

When a relationship has gotten to this stage, couples often try to get back into the routine of having sex. Starting with hand-holding, hugs and kisses, is a more gentle way to reintroduce yourselves to that kind of romantic intimacy, as both partners need to feel comfortable with this level of closeness before they can reintroduce sex into their relationship.

From making out to a simple peck on the lips, when we kiss someone we're in love with, we're not doing it just because it's nice. We're doing it because we have to. **We feel compelled to do it, drawn to them, turned on, comforted, or even simply just seen.**

What kissing does in a relationship is as simple as it is crucial: it connects the two of you. Taking time out to kiss your partner isn't just a way of reconnecting with them, it's a way of reconnecting with yourself. A kiss isn't that different from the relaxation you get after a good session of yoga or meditation. It returns you to your center, restoring you and getting you through your day, reminding you to breathe.

A kiss, even a casual one, becomes an important ritual. **A kiss is a way of marking the space the two of you share together.** Keep in mind that **hugs are great, too**. I strongly encourage any couple who is having a hard time with their physical connection **to incorporate hugs into their routine**. Just understand that a kiss is more powerful and therefore more necessary to the viability of any romantic relationship.

When you stop kissing, you are tacitly agreeing that the romantic portion of your life together is done. There is no need for this to be the case. A hand on the back, a kiss on the head, a little kiss goodbye — these are all easy, sweet ways to reconnect over what brought you together to begin with. The way you kiss each other might change with time, but how the two of you are together kissing should be central to how the two of you connect.

Touching each other is so key to long-term love happiness. We need to be cuddled, touched, loved as when we were a baby. One cannot pay for a kiss, or a simple caring touch. We can pay for cleaning the house, for laundry, for washing dishes.

While going for minor surgery, the reassurance of touching soothes us. We touched the whole time, I adore the warmth of her body, of her hands touching me. Going back to when I was young, I guess I was touched a lot by my mother. And I was probably genetically wired to touch others and to be touched.

102

The best parts of my day are two. First, when I get up in the morning, and we touch, we caress, we hug, we kiss, we say "I love you." Second, when we go to sleep, and we touch, we kiss, we talk, we hug, we caress. The morning routine is invigorating. The evening repetition ensures a good serene sleep. The two together are a strong infusion of love happiness.

Psychiatrics say that the need to touch, to kiss, to cuddle, to hug, to be sexually intimate, really never goes away. My physician implied pretty openly that he at 60 was still making love to his wife, receiving blow jobs, able to touch her anywhere and receiving plenty of tenderness. **Human warmth is clean energy**, as my mother-in-law says ("Calore umano, energia pulita," in Italian).

Hot sex by itself is not secure love, or even love. **Secure attachment leads to hot sex, and also love that lasts.** So good sex by itself cannot lead to long-term satisfying love relationships. **It is the other way around. Not first good sex, then good love. Instead, first good love (empathic emotional altruistic relationship), then good sex.**

It is emotion that defines the quality of the sex we have. An emotion is the quality of our connection to our partner. **The deeper, stronger the emotional connection, the more satisfaction we'll derive from sex**, as we are able to trust our partner and focus wholly on the physical pleasure, enhanced by the emotional connection.

I will never forget when I first heard my wife saying, as she was close to orgasm, "I love you so much." First I must admit I thought she was getting sex and love confused. Then, as I read all the many studies for this book, and reflected on it, I understood that **she was able to get so much physical pleasure from the sexual act because of the intimate emotional bond she felt with me, and understood I had for her**.

In secure attachment we find trust in our partner, and this leads to us giving ourselves completely to our partner, creating true long-lasting passion. In a way, monogamy based on a secure attachment leads to the best long-lasting sex. Attachment determines how we behave in bed as well as out of it.

Feelings of appreciation, tenderness, gratitude, and surrender get translated in a physical act. So wonderful!! **We can drop our guard, and**

be ourselves, even fulfilling our secret dreams of kinky sex and erotic fantasies. Fantasies can become realities. Submission, domination, even some violence, rule-breaking scenarios can become reality if communication – verbal or physical - has allowed mutual trust and acceptance.

To be able to participate in our lover's apparently dirtiest, most private, guiltiest thoughts, frees the couple, makes them reach new heights of emotional bonding. The punishing dichotomy between clean and dirty, good and bad, disappears.

Our greatest strength is to be able to be dependent on our partner, and give ourselves all to them without restrictions and fears. This can only happen when we trust that our partner loves us, i.e. wants us to be happy. **Adult empathic love indeed has been shown in studies to be made of three main elements. The first is attachment. The second is caregiving. The third is sexuality**.

Studies have shown that **contented partners attribute about 15-20% of their happiness to a pleasing sex life. Interestingly, unhappy mates ascribe 50-70% of their distress to sexual problems**.[3] What is really happening is that happy partners connect in many ways, including sex, but not only sex.

What is more important in a positive love relationship than sexuality?? Two other important elements: **caregiving** – which is a blend of attentiveness and empathy, and **attachment** – the emotional connection. Only if we connect well emotionally, can we connect well – and long-term – sexually.

Caregiving is a blend of attentiveness and empathy, being able to assure our partner feels loved, cared for, protected, accepted no matter the idiosyncrasies.

Unhappy couples have lost connection, and sex is the most obvious disconnect. The lack of emotional intimacy leads to physical distance, which is to our conscious much more obvious that the mental disconnect. And this becomes soon a catch 22 situation: no emotional bond, no sex. No sex, even more emotional distance.

Three kinds of sex have been described, in terms of emotional connection. Sealed-off sex, solace sex, and synchrony sex.

104

Sealed-off sex focuses on performance and sensation. It might lead to orgasm, with no or little emotional bond. One partner stays aloof, preferring sex in which arousal and orgasm are ends in themselves, and they want nothing else. Little preliminaries, no after-sex cuddling. "I am a blown-up Barbie for him. Our sex is so empty. I am alone, even if there is physical closeness." Emotional disengagement denies the couple of the richer deeper dimension of sexuality. This is toxic for a love relationship.

Solace sex occurs when we are seeking reassurance that we are valued and desired. The goal is to alleviate our attachment fears. An anxiously-attached person may seek this kind of sex often, "If he desires me, then I feel safe."

Synchrony sex is **when emotional openness and responsiveness, tender touch, and erotic exploration all come together**. This occurs when partners are securely attached. These two secure lovers are **attuned first mentally** with each other, sensing each other inner state and intention, and responding to each others' needs with altruistic passion. One of the best part of this sex for both partners is the after sex, when they hold each other and each feels so precious, so needed, so loved, so appreciated, so understood.

Problems with lovemaking are a major reason people start wondering if their relationship is too bad to stay in. Almost always problems with sexual intimacy are the overt sign of hidden relationship issues. Sex is like those canaries miners carry into a cave to see if the air is safe. Canaries are highly sensitive to lack of oxygen. Sexual problems uncover early relationship problems; sex it's like a way to check how is the atmosphere.

Attachment is most important, for as we connect emotionally, so we connect sexually. Much of this book aims at enhancing the emotional bond between partners. The three different attachment styles influence not only our motives for having sex, but also our sexual performances and satisfaction, and finally the impact of sex on our love relationships.

For example, for people who are **avoidant**, sex is an act aimed at achieving as quickly as possible an orgasm, while minimizing emotional closeness, and even physical closeness, as much as that is possible while having sex. Darkness, silence, no emotions shared, just a pure physical act with little foreplay, preferably no kissing or tender touching at all.

Afterwards, avoidants want **no cuddling, no tender words**, perhaps best instead a quick shower. Partner's feelings must be kept in check, are deemed insignificant, and are promptly dismissed even if hinted at.

The effect of physical intimacy is profound in secure and anxious people, while avoidants do not get an emotional effect, and so sex does not connect the partners intellectually. The beneficial boost of sex does not occur if one partner is avoidant. As the avoidant partner dismisses the attachment significance of sex, the other partners gets alienated. The avoidant partner is determined to stay detached.

A **secure** bond instead is characterized by openness and communication in the bedroom and outside the bedroom. Great sex should be full of chatter, loving words, laughter, play. As the partners feel loved and protected by the other, they have the freedom to explore and be sexually adventurous.

Safety fosters a willingness to experiment, to take risks, and to be fully immersed in the sexual encounter. Sex is more spontaneous, passionate, and joyful. A strong emotional bond leads to good sex, which in turn leads to a still stronger bond, and so on, in a virtuous catch-22 cycle.

Sexual satisfaction and excitement for men, women and LGBTQIA+ increase with emotional commitment and sexual exclusivity.

It is true that men feel arousal more based on looks, and so a miniskirt and long legs on high heels and curvy figure increase blood flow to his penus and cause an erection, sending also a message to his brain that ,"I want sex with this person."

For over 90% of men everywhere in the world, the length of the penus during an erection is about 10-18 cm, more less 4-7 inches.[8] The vagina is 8-13 cm long, so even a smaller penus can reach deep. During penetration, women's pleasure is apparently more linked to the penus' diameter than to its length.

As so many studies have shown, the shape or other characteristics of the vagina or penus are not linked much to sexual pleasure, to orgasm:

the brain, and its related sense of sensual intimacy, are the factors most associated with sexual satisfaction.

For women, in general, sex is more of a combination of physical and emotional feelings. For women sexual desire is also a search for feeling safe, protected, as research shows. Women feel lust, just as much as men; but they quickly pair it with safety concerns.

This makes sense anthropologically. Sex is a lot riskier for women. They can get pregnant with each sexual encounter, and the pregnancy can put their life at risk. Even in 2024, about a woman every 5,000 in high-income countries, and 1 in 50 in low- and middle-income countries, dies of pregnancy.[26]

Interestingly, when the decision to have sex appears in our brain, only in women, and not in men, does the prefrontal cortex and other cerebral regions involved in making judgements and decisions illuminate on functional MRIs. For some men instead, what Woody Allen said probably fits, "Sex without love is a meaningless experience, but as meaningless experiences go, it's pretty darn good."

Watching porn, more common in men, can also generate physical pleasure and an orgasm. So does using a vibrator for women. Studies show that a screen- or machine-generated orgasm triggers the pleasure chemicals endorphins, dopamine, and serotonin. It does not, however, discharge oxytocin, the attachment hormone.

One of the reasons why women have more oxytocin receptors than men may be that this stress-reducing hormone helps to turn off their fears, and so allows them to have less anxious sex. Oxytocin lets many women have a more emotional, brain-happy, not-only-genital-happy, sex.

Men should be aware that innumerous studies show that women's sexuality depends on the quality of the relationship and the safety feeling just as much if not more than the intensity of the sensations coming from her skin and her body. Men should therefore be smart to adjust their verbal and physical approaches to make it apparent that there is desire for the person, not just for sex.

The woman wants to be desired as a human being, not only as a vagina. Men who share their feelings have a lot more success in getting women to agree to sex. Another notion men should acquire is that while they (men) would feel good by making their partner have an orgasm, women feel satisfied with a sexual encounter at times even without having an orgasm. This is so different than men. But proven scientifically in many studies.

Attachment and sex are supposed to go together in our physiology, usually. Those who try to only have sex without feelings often become addicted, to multiple encounters with different people (e.g. prostitutes, etc), or with other means such as video or toy stimulation.

And like other addictions (e.g. tobacco, drugs), we often need more and more of it, getting less and less satisfied as our dopamine receptors get used to the dopamine release, and our sex-without-brain becomes less and less fulfilling.

Sex is usually the search for a secure attachment, and failing to find some emotional oxytocin-lead pleasure leads to ever less satisfying sex. Interestingly, other addictions such opioid use disorder are, at the base, desperate attempts to find a substitute for secure attachment to others.

Some call it 'soul sex.' This occurs when physical pleasure is accompanied by an exchange of tender words. It's the best when a partner says, **"I love you" during sex, during an orgasms, during multiple orgasms**. It is a total thrill, of body and soul. It's like a morning sun rising, and warming every part of our being. **When we bring attachment and sex together, there is nothing better, and we do achieve love happiness**.

A key to understand, in particular for a man, if there is love associated with the sex, is how he feels after ejaculation. If there is no love, he wants to leave, wants to flee, wants to free himself from her and from the whole circumstances which led to the sex.

It's a situation not too dissimilar from hunger, or thirst. Once we are full, or no longer thirsty, the left-over food goes back in the fridge, we get up and leave the dining table. In fact some males feel the naked body of the woman next to them as fastidious after sex.

If instead the man is in love, he wants to still stay close, hug the object of his desire and also his affection, he wants more intimacy, more connection, now in a more platonic and empathic way.

Studies and surveys have shown that good sex can last indefinitely with one partner. Actually, with time, a secure bond allows each other to share more and more our preferences, and therefore allows our partner to make us ever more pleasurably satisfied during sex.

Sexuality is **indispensable**. For most of us, it is as important as food, water, the air we breathe. Often sexual problems are the tip of the iceberg of relationship problems. A long-term relationship who still finds comfort in physical touch and sex, is seldom unhappy.

Sex should also be a game. A way of playing with each other. **A way to renew our knowledge of each other. Adults often quit playing. Become too serious**. They do not want to explore novelties. They do not enjoy freedom, but embrace routine, which is so boring! Adults should bring more joy, curiosity, freedom in the bedroom (and outside!).

What's **most exciting, for example, is to make your partner experience sexual pleasure**. The fact that she is aroused, almost on drugs from the ecstasy you can see in the other's face and body, is the best aphrodisiac. Again, all in the brain, in what's between our ears. And certainly eyes - sight, ears - hearing, nose - smell, mouth - taste, help as much as touch as far as sex is concerned.

The most joy in sex is making your partner squeal from hallucinogenic pleasure. Men get hardest when their partner is enjoying being physically together to the point of passing out from the brain being inundated by gleeful chemicals. **A lover who enjoys what you do to them is a better aphrodisiac than anything else in life**.

When **she says "I love you" as she was having an orgasm**, you should not think that as awkward, as if he has mistaken love and sex. Good sex is better when in love. Sex can feed love. Love can feed sex. The two together are more than just the sum. Saying "I love you" sincerely during sex is reaching the emotional sky of love happiness.

It's important to also be cognizant of some other data. Since Masters and Johnson, and before then even, we have known that **desire is the first step** towards a possible consensual sexual encounter. Desire often, as we have seen, stems from intellectual intimacy, and so the brain is clearly our most important sexual organ. Then follow arousal, orgasm, and satisfaction.

109

Research shows that 1 in 3 women and 1 in 7 men report inhibited sexual desire. Even in married couples, more that 50% of partners report either inhibited desire or desire discrepancy. One in 5 marriages have sex less than 10 times a year. Another 15% of couples have sex less than every other week, or less than 26 times a year.[27]

The average number of times a couple has sex is about 1-2 per week. **Most couples have a sexual frequency of between once every 2 weeks to 2-3 times a week.** One or two satisfying – emotionally and physically - sexual encounters a month should be considered a healthy positive experience. This is considered normal, based on scientific data.

Indeed, **quality is more important than quantity**. Being able to give oneself openly and fully to the sexual encounter, with the aim to make the other partner happy the way she likes to, is a lot more satisfying than a 5-minute brute act leading to a quick but intellectually-empty orgasm.

Fatal flaws in a happy heterosexual or homosexual relationship are a hidden sexual life outside the two partners, marrying for convenience and security without genuine feeling for the partner, and keeping extra affairs outside the relationship. Another fatal flow for couples is when one member is a heterosexual in an homosexual relationship, or an homosexual in an heterosexual relationship, or in general sexual desires do not match.

The bond instead should be based on trust, honesty, and communication. Disclosing secrets, preferences, passions, facilitates successful erotic exchanges.

Anger towards the partner can create a sexuality wall. Not doing the laundry by the male partner may cause the female partner to lose sexual desire. Anger can also stem from one partner, often the male, wanting an orgasm from every encounter.

The women sense first hurt and disappointment at just feeling as a sexual object, and then **anger when they feel powerless to have, at least sometimes, touching and cuddling without intercourse and orgasm**.

Touching should be valued for itself, and caressing and sweet exchanges of words should be frequent and not always lead to intercourse.

It is quite normal that at least 5-15% of sexual encounters, even between usually successful partners, are mediocre, disappointments, or failures.

Keeping it real is another important consideration. The average time for intercourse from **intromission to ejaculation is 2 to 7 minutes**. Less than 10% of intercourse episodes last more than 10 minutes. Lovemaking usually lasts 15-45 minutes, mostly in foreplay and desire, as well as postcoital closeness.

Unfortunately media makes us believe an erection can last so much longer; it usually doesn't, and it's only natural, nobody's fault. Ejaculation controlling exercises do work, especially the start-and-stop technique, in which the male signals he is close to ejaculation, and things are allowed to slow down, or stop completely for a few minutes. But these can only delay orgasm a few minutes at most.

The **presence and number of orgasms** does not correlate directly with partners' satisfaction. A **third of women do not have orgasms during intercourse**. Five to ten percent of women has never experienced orgasm by any means. Most women do not have an orgasm at each sexual opportunity, and are still quite happy with non-orgasmic sex. One in four have usually one orgasm per encounter. About **20% are capable of having multiple orgasms**.

Even more important for you to know, is that studies have shown that **about 30% of women say they have little or no desire for sex**, even with a committed, loving partner, while **about 15% of men report feeling little desire**.[3]

Unfortunately research shows also that **up to 90% of people have had negative sexual encounters in the past**. Being able to discuss these as necessary, seeking professional help if needed, and being able to get past the fears, is of paramount importance.

Few people fantasize about intercourse in bed in the missionary position. If individuals were prosecuted for their sexual thoughts and fantasies, we'd be all in jail. Sexual fantasies are natural, healthy, and should be shared with our partner. Accept your partner's wishes. And remember than you do not have to prove any sexual amazing prowess or disinhibition to demonstrate yourself as a more than satisfactory sexual lover to your partner.

Some make the analogy between sex and ice cream. Some have 2 or 3 preferred flavors, which they choose regularly. Some want to try all 35 flavors, at different times. Please 'marry' into your partner preferences. There is nothing wrong about 3 or 33 preferred flavors, or preferred ways to have sex.

Another key element to a healthy sexual relationship is a **regular rhythm of sexual contact, whether twice a week or every 10 days**. If neglected, enthusiasm goes away, and desire dies. **If after 2 weeks there has been no intimate encounter, it's best that one of the partners initiates some touching**, cuddling, common-shower, or other desire-stimulating activity to keep the flame alive.

While sex should be spontaneous, it does help to put it up on our schedule, and if need be, please have an understood agreed-on routine. Saturday evening dinner out together often will be accompanied back home by sex. Or Tuesday morning. Or more frequently when we go on vacation. And so on.

Requests and expectations regarding sex should be reasonable for the other partner. Realistic expectations, and not just some unrealistic thing we saw on tv or social media, are important to share. No couple has the perfect sexual life, or the perfect relationship. Do not compare your intimate life to that of actors on tv or hearsay from other couples.

Here too, regarding sex this time, most important is to **know our own wishes well, as well as our partner preference**s. You and your partner are each unique individuals; choose what fits you two best. After these wishes and preferences are openly shared, the couple should develop agreements between each other that nurture desire first, and sexuality to follow.

Think of the issue of sex a bit like we did regarding attachment styles. Know your preferred sexual preferences, and your partner's sexual preferences. Work to make them more compatible, and to accept differences, that are inevitable. To be different is not only normal but to be expected.

If your partner dislikes sex, and/or never has orgasms, and in general disdains seeking desire as they are avoidant of any intimacy, emotional and/or physical, it's important you discover these traits sooner rather than later. If you are a physical person with secure emotional needs for bodily intimacy, this partner may not work for you, and you better be honest to him and to yourself, to avoid decades of heartache.

Our problems escalate when we do not discuss issues deeply, openly. Her desire for sex increases also because the need it's being denied. **A pleasure denied is a pleasure intensified**. Meanwhile he finds his sexual desire decreasing because of her pressure. Attempts at solving the difference in needs may actually at times escalate the issue itself.

The main aphrodisiac is an involved, aroused partner. There is nothing more stimulating than a partner full of desire. **The issue at times is initiating the sexual encounters. Some of us are less prone to be the initiator**. And if both partners are shy or lazy about the first step, then no-sex will be the results for quite some time, or forever.

Sharing feelings, reliving the daily experiences together, being affectionate, cuddling on the couch or in bed, disclosing hopes and fears, touching, dancing, giving each other a massage are all excellent examples of how to **build trust and initiate desire**.

It's therefore best at times to allow sensual and sexual touching to occur at the woman's pace, rather than at the man's. Communicating feelings and preferences is so important. Many women prefer indirect, rather than direct clitoral stimulation. Again, most important is for the woman to know her preferences. Then she must share them openly and kindly with her partner.

Ultimately, **satisfaction with sex is scientifically proven to be more linked to emotional satisfaction, than to the number or frequency of orgasm**. Sexuality does not have to be the top priority in a relationship, but should be a positive, integral component.

Intimacy dates range from a walk and talk, time on the porch over a drink, a night out for dinner and/or a movie, dancing, having a bubble bath together, soaping each other's back naked in the shower, planning a vacation together, watching an erotic movie, putting your favorite soul music on, or many other activities.

Perhaps a good plan for you is for one partner initiating once a week her own intimacy date – say walking and talking after a long day at work, and the other week the man initiates it – say ballroom dancing class.

Contrary to cultural myths, women value sexuality as much as men. The core to sexuality is giving and receiving pleasure-oriented touching.

There are a myriad of scientific, comprehensive, helpful books and online materials regarding sex. This book just wanted to cover the basics of how to make sexuality a healthy part of love happiness.

Factors associated with a successful long-term relationship

I like my work; I love my wife.

In 'Trains, planes, and automobiles'

Happy wife, Happy life

There are a few factors which love relationship science has found be fundamentals to achieve long-term love happiness (Table 7). Here are the details.

Effective frequent communication[28]

Consider that great love relationships and life goals are risky: if you lose, cherish the lesson anyway. Being surrounded by love at home should be the base for your life. When you disagree with the ones you love, stick to the current issue. Do not bring back old arguments.

Dalai Lama

The two persons in a romantic love relationship should be **best friends, and confidants**. They want to be together to share thoughts, experiences. They know each other intimately, being well versed in each other's likes, dislikes, idiosyncrasies, as well as personal hopes and dreams. The connection must be deep, a total understanding. This can only be based on trust and commitment.

The authors of the '7 principles' book call this 'enhancing your love maps.'[28] **Each lover should want to really get to know in the most profound specifics the details of his partner's life**. Her background. Her upbringing. Her most notable life experiences. Her life at work. Her friends. Her dreams. Her goals. Her fears. Her likes. Her stresses.

Emotionally connected couples are **intimately familiar with each other's world**. They know their partner's best friends' names and main issues. They have made a conscious effort to make cognitive space for everything that their partner cares about. It's impossible to truly love without first knowing. In fact, **'to know' in biblical terms is 'to have sex,' as even the ancients knew that mental intimacy leads to better physical connections**.

A question that should be answered sooner rather than later in a crucial love conversation is, "**What am I most afraid of?**" And in fact don't be afraid to ask, when your partner is clearly in distress, "What are you most afraid could happen?" I have been flabbergasted to hear at times that a partner would be afraid of the other leaving her, if he did not compliment her clothes more often. What may look to one partner as frivolous or unimportant, may mean the world to the other.

Being able to **stay connected with the present events in the other's life** is paramount. That is why at least an hour of quality time a day to unwind to each other minds, and a weekly dinner out together, are so important. Just to talk. We need to feel known and understood by our love partner. To know another human being well is to love her.

Your goal is to **listen and learn. When you are together, ask open-ended questions**, like, "How would you like your life to be different three years from now?" Or, "What was keeping you up last night?"; "How come you raised your voice a bit on the phone with your mother?"

This **hunger for safe emotional connection is a survival imperative we experience from cradle to grave. Love that starts as a true selfless friendship, given kinship of attitudes and interest, is a love that has a good chance to last long**.

Too many people play instead a guessing game with their partner. Like when we were babies and we expected our mother to realize our need, we expect our partner to read our mind. Instead, **if we want something as adults, we should just ask for it.**

We should be honest and straightforward. "I do not like the way you flirted with that girl. Can you be less friendly? Some may misunderstand you." Or, "Sorry to tell you this, but your breath smells. Can please you brush your teeth?"

Anytime your partner asks you to do something, be open to it. Do not take it as a personal criticism, but as a chance to grow, to get

to a better version of yourself. In meeting the needs of your partner, you'll be improving yourself – a better breath and clean gums and teeth improve your health; if a partner has some degree of healthy jealousy, it means after all that she still loves you.

There are whole books dedicated solely to communication, so I'll give just the highlights here. Do it. Every day, talk more than 1 hour with each other. A recent fMRI study found that just being able to put feelings into words seems to calm our painful and difficult emotions. Take turns, and give each other 15 minutes to vent about each other's day.

Show genuine interest. Don't even give advice; your partner does not want solutions, just wants to talk to try to better understand herself how to improve the situation. Don't do something, just be there. You have two ears and one mouth, and that should be the minimal ratio between listening and talking when your partner needs to communicate something to you. Minimal; perhaps 4:1 or 8:1 would be better ratios in some situations.

Communicate instead your understanding of the situation, so she knows you have been listening attentively. Take her side. Express a 'we against them' attitude, as you are a united team against outside threats. Show affection. Validate emotions.

One needs to truly put oneself in the partner's shoes, see the situation from the partner's point of view, by intensely listening. One must learn to accept the partner's view of the world. Our partner's view is just as true as our view. Yes we can also share data and facts. But emotionally we must be able to create some common view more valid than either of us can create alone.

Hopefully the best scenario would be that we both give something up, only to gain a great deal more together. And each successful understanding creates a bit of a stronger bond in our love relationship.

Three important steps to successful communication are mirroring, validation, and empathy.

Mirroring involves communicating to our partner back what she is telling us. This is key to helping our partner feel heard and loved. Mirroring encourages the partner to communicate even more intimate feelings, so the listening partner can most deeply understand the speaking partner's troubles. It's a necessary luxury to have a partner who we truly believe is listening to us.

As a partner responds empathically to the other, research has shown that specific nerve cells, called **mirror neurons**, are activated in the prefrontal cortex. **These neurons allow us to actually feel what someone else is feeling**. Authentic connection is about 'feeling felt.' Two people are now in **emotional synchrony**, without conscious thought or spoken word.

There is calmness and joy. In these moments, our brain is also flooded with oxytocin. Giving humans oxytocin increases the tendency to trust and interact with others. We are all different, with some having more or less oxytocin in their brain, or more or less oxytocin receptors. Oxytocin seems to be nature's way of promoting attachment.

Validation involves that the listening partner communicates back that he **concurs with the speaking partner's view**, and even with her feelings. We share that, "I can see why you see it this way. I can understand why you have these feelings." We may not have reacted the way our partner did to the situation she faced, but we understand it's quite all right that our partner did. Our partner wants us to make her feel that she is not crazy.

It's key to abandon a view centered only on our beliefs and feelings, and instead to embrace as possible and human and quite normal to react and think the way our partner does. Once we are willing to see and accept a different point of view, this liberates the discussion. It allows for open communication, and deeper sharing.

Empathy involves the **understanding of the feelings of the partner**. Given the issues, the listening partner fully endorses to the speaking partner that her feelings are normal, expected, valid, and they make sense. When our feelings are empathically shared by our partner, the souls get closer, united. Any possible anger or misunderstanding dissipates once we feel fully acknowledged and validated in acts and feelings.

Communication also requires **energy, and time**. There is effort required into being good listeners when needed. And lots of time needs to be dedicated to truly understanding and supporting our partner, as she shares her emotions with us, the lucky ones to be given a window into our lovers' souls.

Being empathic towards our loved one greatly helps communication. The partner listening really listens, and in his brain forms a clear image - *seeing* his partner - of what the other is feeling, and even experiences the sensations the other is communicating - feelings of pain, fear, mistrust, whatever. The **listening lover is able to *mirror in his mind* the emotional response the other is going through.**

The mirroring is not only in the brain, but also in the body, and in words. As our partner communicated disgust, the listening partner *mimics* the response with his body, for example by cringing at the same time as his partner. Word mirroring and repeating the partner in distress help communicate true understanding, and *sharing* that we also feel the pain, the suffering.

The listening partner knows that she knows that he understands. The other partner feels heard, understood, and emotionally supported. This is what mental intimacy is.

Love reaches a pitch when our beloved turns out to **understand us better than anyone else in the world.** Our partner **should understand us better sometimes than even our own chaotic self.** Our partner sympathizes and forgives us like nobody else can in the world. We can reveal our own mind in its entirety with our love partner, without secrets.

This is where two people can become truly **soul-mates.** Share secrets with each other. A childhood memory. A feeling about your parents. A vivid dream. Telling someone something reveals something about yourself. **So in a sense communication is a process of getting naked. Not physically, but mentally, interpersonally. And love has to be the place where it's safe to be naked.**

The person in love likes to bear all, to open up completely, to keep no secrets, to finally unload to her trustworthy and empathic partner. The partner who is not in love keeps secrets, he does not reveal his soul. This is another way to gauge if your partner is truly into you or not.

Part of the experience of falling in love and being in love is taking off all the masks, and revealing yourself in full. It means **relaxing into feeling safer the more naked you get.** You find safety by baring it all.

119

You become vulnerable but more loveable. Your getting naked naturally and fully provides safety for your partner to also be herself. The more your partner accepts and joins in the mental nakedness, the more two souls can caress each other.

As a partner, **when you chose a mate, look for vulnerability**. **Someone in love is vulnerable. Someone who pretends to be in love but isn't, is instead strong, void of intimate emotions**. It's sad to see when we 'fall' for the tough dudes, and reject the 'weak' shy dudes who can hardly talk a straight sentence as they are so lost in love.

Too many people hide themselves to their partner. Why we act a certain way often depends from prior experiences, as a child and as an adult. For example, there is a reason why we have fear of sharing certain feelings. Perhaps our parents were not warm, not open with their own feelings, and we never learned how to share our true emotions.

We should at least at some point early in the relationship share this aspect of our life. We need to make sure our partner understands we might be tight-lipped because of what happened in our past, not because we do not love them.

Our partner then should be honored to receive the insight, and eager to work together to allow some sharing of feelings going forward. Suddenly the receiving partner gets a major glimpse into the 'shy' partner, and understands what the constrained partner was going through.

An important part of love is just **gratitude for our lover's insight** into our own confused and troubled psyche. Our lover's acceptance ends loneliness and shame. We now live through our partner in a world of encouragement and approval, of acceptance and support.

This understanding **reaches its peak when it is spontaneous, when our partner understands our needs before we even communicate these needs**. This longing for unspoken understanding goes back to the womb and to our early childhood.

In the womb, food and warmth and protection were given to us without asking. Our every requirement was catered for. Even in our first year of life, large caring people around us guessed what we needed, and so changed our diaper, fed us good things such as breast milk, put us in the crib when we were tired.

We as adults feel certain that we are genuinely understood only when we do not have to say or explain what we need. Just like when we were fetuses or infants. Deep inside, the infant has remained in us, and we need our partner to **correctly guess what we need now, without asking, just like when we were a baby**.

So we shouldn't have to ask for a caress, a massage, a kind word, the laundry to be started, grocery shopping to be done. When we might not be in our best mood, we hope our partner will ask us why. Actually, even better would be for our partner to know why we are upset even without asking, just like our mother did when we cried as babies. Some of us actually remain more of an inarticulate child than others.

We must train ourselves to be to others what they need us to be for them, even before our partner knows she might have a want. We should comprehend the true need of our lover even better than our lover understands it herself. We need to bring things out of our partner to help them.

Making your inner world available to your partner, and as importantly helping our partner via communication share his world with you, will greatly strengthen your relationship. An excellent way to improve between-partners communication is to discover each other's strengths. You and your partner should **take the Gallup Strength Survey today!**[14]

I discovered many years ago through this simple survey that my number one strength is Learner. My wife is a Learner, too. We have many other top strengths, and we know them about each other. We also know that in particular five strengths have been shown to be associated with flourishing. These are love, gratitude, zest, hope, and curiosity. These are hugely important in a relationship.

It's so important to **communicate each other's needs**. "I would love a back rub." "Let's have a dinner date every week as possible." "Can you help more with the laundry?" We can't have it all, but we can teach our partner what would be our most important desire. Not the 10 most important desires. Stick to simplicity, and start with one.

This is hard work, indeed. Studies show that about 70% of the time even happily bonded mothers and infants miss each other's signals.[3] It's

121

about the same in loving couples; we just get distracted, we are not 'in the moment,' our emotional ears are temporarily deaf. It's impossible to always stay in tune with our partner. We should strive to be aligned at least most of the time, even better than our mother did with us.

Interestingly, **many partners have similar needs**, even if often this is not overly clear to them. When the partner is able to overcome the initial resistance and fulfill the wish/need of the other partner, often a part of his unconscious mind interprets his caring behavior as self-directed, as the happiness in his partner makes himself happy.

He can interpret the back rub he is giving to his partner as pleasurable to himself, as he gets to touch his partner, he gets some exercise, etc. Love of the self is achieved through love of the other. And a happier partner will for sure make our own life happier. When you are able to become more generous and loving to your spouse, therefore, your brain assumes that the activity is intended to make you happy too.

The last step in this sequence of effective empathic communication is being able to respond to the lover in distress on an emotional level, and so being able **finally to actually *help*.** "What do I need most from you?" is a crucial question, a tipping point. It helps so much that the distressed partner feels deeply that her pain actually hurts her lover, too.

The distressed lover needs to also be open to receiving all these 'helpful' empathic signals from the supporting partner. Her mirror neurons need to be alert; she needs to perceive the signals of support despite anxiety, pain, depression; she needs not to be distracted.

Sometimes two people just end up disagreeing on an issue, an event. The scientific advice is to keep this between the couple. It's best to agree in public, in front of in-laws, or friends, or kids. "Let's do as your father says." "Your mother is always right." It's best to leave the longer discussions for one-on-one sessions.

Some arguments cannot be solved, even in private. Sometimes members of a couple need to just agree to disagree, amicably. Many marital arguments cannot be resolved exactly how we would want them. A husband raised with a live-in nanny who cleaned constantly after him will probably never routinely do the laundry.

Best is to accept it, to push so he does help occasionally in this or other house tasks, and get outside help if we do not want to do laundry most of the time. After the disagreement is agreed on, we need to learn to live with it, still honoring and respecting each other.

Emotional connection

Wherever we are together, that's my home.

The **ability to tune in our partner when he shares his deeper feelings**, and to **share emotional moments of mental intimacy**, sits at the top of the love happiness pyramid (Figure 3). The depth and frequency of emotional bonding events are directly correlated to the success of the relationship. That is, the more of these emotional moments, the more the relationship is predicted to be satisfactory and positive years later.

Love needs us to **enjoy each other's company**. Love is **companionship**. It's important to want to spend quality time with our partner. It's important to savor our partner and our time with them. This could be whispering something sweet as we wake up. Spontaneously embracing her from behind. Listening to his troubles at work.

The best and most beautiful things in the world cannot be seen or even touched, **they are felt with the heart. Being together with our loved one should bring joy by itself,** even if we are just taking our routine evening walk holding hands in our favorite park or part of town. And this precious time together is best filled with touching, compliments, loving phrases towards each other, gratitude, appreciation.

We should crave to savor our time together with our partner.[29] Savoring then takes us to mindfulness, to experience flow together, to a meta-awareness that goes behind the superficial experience of things and events.

Savoring means putting the time together with our partners first. We look forward to nothing less than a quiet evening together with our partner, with a simple dinner and our favorite wine, just sharing our day and our emotions. Wishing nothing else, desiring nothing more, with no interruptions, with no phones, no internet, no tv.

For me, it's amazing what emotional deep connection does to my inside wellness, and how I look at my daily activities. **If I am with a loving positive partner, I enjoy even activities which I generally disliked, such as shopping**. Everything becomes pleasurable and fun when done together.

We should be each other's best friends. **The ability to listen to the other** is often what makes the other person fall in love with us. The ability to really listen and understand what the other is saying. To be able not to interrupt. To be able not to judge. **To be able not to just counter our story to their story**. But to concentrate and focus on her story only.

We are designed to deal with emotions and feelings in concert with another person, both genetically and since we were young and shared openly with our parents. **The myth that we should sort our emotions first inside by ourselves is negated by the recent scientific evidence. Two hearts, and indeed two minds, are better than one**.

We do know that **team work always achieves better results than a single member**. I learned this at Harvard myself in 2002, at a leadership course. Despite being with 45 leaders in our field, our individual results were always inferior to those of teams of 4 to 9 of us.

The best predictor of which NBA team was going to win the final playoffs in 2008-2009 was the number of times team members reached for and touched each other in the first game! We humans were made to be together, and do better together. There is no better team than two partners in empathic love.

One mate usually falls in love not as much with what we say; even if certainly that is important. She falls in love even more with our positive, active ability to listen. So in a way they fall in love more with our ears, than with our mouth.

Savoring should involve often **expressing our love to our partner**. Having our partner stating out loud how much he loves us, is wonderful. We need to spontaneously, honestly share with our partner that we relish the joy of loving her. We need to express our love often, openly, directly.

And these expressions of love should be reciprocal. Then they cause a spiral of positivity. This is *affective affirmation.*

Couples can interact within themselves and with the outside world in very different ways. According to a Swiss study, there are 5 types of couples.[8] These are:

- Allied Couple (24%): Social life is the main trait of these couples. These two may be high school or college sweethearts, who have a nice social life with close friends, with their kids' families, with their respective original families, and still like each other too.
- Trench Couple (16%): Members of this couple have very separate tasks: one cooks, another cleans, another is the main earner, with fixed routines, and an aversion for change and surprises. The status quo rules.
- Refuge Couple (15%): These are home bodies, who like to do little things at home, or at the same vacation house, without much interactions with others outside the two members of the couple.
- Associative Couple: This couple has different hobbies, different goals in life. They share the roof, the bed, the kitchen, expenses, but individual aims are more important than couple aims, of which there are none, or very few.
- Parallel Couple: The members of this couple live completely different lives. They have given up on love, common goals, common pleasures, love happiness. In the weekend he plays golf, she spends time with her girlfriends. Work is his main goal, or hers, or both.

The healthier couple, the one with more hope for love happiness, is the Allied Couple. One can certainly survive in couples of other types, but in these it's harder to achieve true love happiness that benefits both us as well as others.

Emotional connection, the basis of companionship, has three main components:[12]

- Accessibility: **Can I reach you?**

- Responsiveness: **Can I rely, count on you** to respond to me emotionally?
- Engagement: Do I know **you will value me and stay close**? I need to know **I matter to you** above all others.

We need to create moments of engagement and connection. We need to have set times alone as a couple. A weekly dinner out. Thirty minutes upon waking up, kissing each other good morning, holding each other, hugging. Leaving short notes, love messages, videos to each other throughput the day. Thirty minutes of real communication each evening. A walk in the park most days, for at least an hour. A vacation together, just the two of you, at least every year. A debrief after work upon returning home from work, looking each other in the eyes, and listening, truly.

Sadly, research has shown that **partners in an American couple spend an average of 12 minutes a day talking to each other**.

Hollywood moments of true connections need to be created daily. In fact, they should become routine. Rituals engage us emotionally. Celebrate birthdays, anniversaries, religious events, accomplishments, in a certain, private unique way, together.

A true conversation 'Hold Me Tight,' as per Sue Johnson,[12] is the ultimate bridge spanning the space of two human beings. She listed what we need to feel to have intense emotional connection:
- I am special to you and you really value our relationship. I am reassured I am number one with you, and for you, and nothing is more important to you than us.
- I am wanted by you, as a partner and as a lover, and making me happy is important to you.
- I am loved and accepted, with my failures and imperfections. You accept that I cannot be perfect, even when I try to.
- I am needed by you. You want me close.
- I am safe because you care about my feelings, hurts, and needs.
- I can count on you to be there for me, and to not leave me alone when I need you.
- I am heard and respected. You do not dismiss me. You give us a chance to grow and improve together.

- I can count on you to hear me and to put everything else aside when I talk and need you.
- I can ask you to hold me and to understand that is a basic human need for me, like air and water.

The word **emotion comes from the Latin 'e-movere,' to move out, forward**. The emotions we feel is what motivates us to do something, to act, to change, to seek. Emotions also are our strongest way of communicating.

It takes one hundred milliseconds for our brain to register the smaller alteration in another person's face. And it takes **just three hundred milliseconds more to feel in our own body what we see in that face**. Our right side seems to be the 'feelings' part of our brain.

We are 'moved' when we deeply connect with another human being. We take risks in sharing, but have a chance to 'love' through 'emotions' bringing the other closer to us. We get both naked, standing face to face, reaching for each other, stronger together.

Studies show that even just being able to name our deep emotions to another human being calms us down, and makes us less anxious, more clear mentally, more positive, more able to then move on and resolve our emotions especially when they are difficult ones to handle.

Suppressing emotions, a behavior unfortunately promoted throughout history, only exacerbates them, like trying to cup a volcano which wants to erupt. The most functional way to regulate difficult emotions is to share them. We should **learn to swim in the river of our feelings and emotions** and share them as we need to.

The better you are at listening to and distilling your emotions and then sending out your emotional signals to your partner, the better your relationship will be. A fMRI study found that just being able to put feelings into words seems to calm our painful and difficult emotions.

Most social scientists list six innate and universal emotions: fear, anger, happiness or joy, surprise, and shame – some divide shame into disgust and guilt. **Fear** seems to be the most powerful of all emotions. The amygdala is the main processing center for fear, and an important decider of our actions and social interactions. Unhappy partners are often visibly angry, but the anger is usually secondary to a deeper sense of fear.

The inability to show emotions completely leaves our lovers lost in ignorance land. There is no signal, no music, no dance, no relationship. It's important to recognize when we are distant. Some people, guys in particular, stay away from the feeling stuff, and know deep down that they are distant and at times emotionally unapproachable.

They need to acknowledge that; may be their parental examples were the same, distant and low-emotional. They need to change though if they want a shot at love happiness. And change starts with recognizing our shortcomings.

Historically, emotions have been described as some opposite of intelligence. Even the ancient Greek philosophers advised to keep emotions in check. **Actually one could argue that emotions are a form, and perhaps a higher form, of intelligence**.

In fact, studies argue that in life 'brain' intelligence, for example an high IQ (Intelligence Quotient), is much less important for happiness and personal success than Emotional Intelligence, EQ (Emotional Quotient Intelligence).

Commitment to each other[28]

You and me, babe, against the world.

Partners should **turn towards each other** and commit deeply to each other's well-being. While life demands their attention in many directions, the main focus should be the happiness of their lover. Partners should spontaneously gravitate towards each other. They should naturally want to **help and support each other.**

A partner always needs help. With a back rub. Or with helping a sick parent. The deed may be small or big; it always needs full attention of the loving partner. When a partner asks for our help, we are committed to be there. No matter the sacrifice. If it means losing the golf outing, or missing watching the Sixers game, so be it: we'll support the partner who needs a walk together to air out work-related grievances.

Scientific research has shown that couples who remain happily together turns towards each other 86% of the time the partner asks for help. Instead, those who end up splitting, turn towards each other only 33% of the time.[28]

Turning towards and helping our partner is like putting money in the love bank. The receiving partner feels recognized, cared for, loved. This is why we need to teach our kids that mom and dad won't be the most important people in their lives once they become adults. They need to put their love partner on the #1 spot in their lives, in every aspect.

So do not miss a 'bid' for help from your partner because of work, being busy, other family members or friends. Your partner, with few occasional temporary exceptions which can be agreed on by your partner, should be #1, in particular when she is asking for support.

Do not be dissuaded by a prior disagreement. By your iPhone or social media. It's so stupid to ignore each other's emotional needs out of mindlessness, not even malice. You'll regret it long term, as **every unmet need corrodes a bit of what you have built so beautifully so far**.

We need to be able to cope with our partner's sadness, fear, anger.[28] A partner needs to be able to stop and be close to the other when the other is in pain. The world should stop, and he should just listen and support. The goal is to care, to pay attention, to understand. It is not to judge, or to give advice.

It's equally important to respond adequately to our partners' good news. **A partner's promotion, award, achievement, must be felt like our own**. The happiness our partner feels, should become our own happiness.

Celebrations are in order. Respond supportively to good news, even if you know this might mean some minor negativity – e.g. our partner might travel for work a bit more. What makes our partner happy, should in general make us happy, as long as our partnership is first and foremost the most important goal for both partners.

Do not ask, "Why?" Ask instead, "What makes you think that?" Or "Help me understand better that issue." You should respect your partner's experiences. And especially her feelings. It helps often to just repeat what your partner is saying, to make sure that there is mutual understanding. Your partner should get that you have been listening and that you comprehend the core facts and feelings. Do not even try to cheer up your partner; accept their moment of sadness.

In fact, seldom it's **ok to accept some anger from the partner** too, as long as it does not reach to the level of insulting us. Communication is so important that if we are angry about an issue, an event, we should communicate, keeping emotion – another common one is fear of being misunderstood - in check but also sharing our feelings.

Do not minimize the issue your partner is struggling with. And do not tell her to calm down. Some people just need to vent for a bit. I guess another name for this key to success is **being empathic**. Your long-term goal should be to learn and improve your sympathy and compassion skills, in particular towards your partner.

Our partner should **feel unique** to us. You need to be the only one he calls, "Darling," "My love," "Amore," "Mon amour." **There is an exclusivity**: nobody could take his place. The partner is inimitable.

Good communication, companionship, and commitment, lead to a **sense of having created a safe nest**. A nest is a place where we feel safe, loved, taken care of. Some researchers have called this concept of nesting also cocooning, another safe intimate place where we can defend ourselves from the stresses of our life outside. A cocoon is probably too closed to the outside. We need to interact with others at some point. A nest is a better description of how we feel with someone we are really in love with, and loved by.

Fostering admiration towards each other[28]

There is only one woman who makes me feel like more than I am.

Another key to love happiness is to **nurture mutual admiration and fondness**. We should have a firm belief that our partner is a person worthy of honor and respect. We should acknowledge consciously the multiple important virtues present in the partner which make him wanted, and therefore the partnership desirable. People who are happily married, like each other, spontaneously, and without much rational effort.

Empathic love involves admiration for qualities in our lover that promise to correct our own weaknesses and imbalances. **Love is a search for personal completion**. Initially we might admire being tall and having broad shoulders in our partner, to protect us and as traits to pass on to our kids. Much more importantly, long-term love success should be tied to admiring honesty, sincerity, and even being neat, being hard-working, being cuddly, or whatever other virtue we long for and make us complete.

Couples who **put a positive spin in their views of their partners** have a 94% chance of having success at love happiness.[28] It's noticing the small things, everyday moments. "I love it when you make the table for the family in such a loving caring way;" "Thanks for making my sister feel welcome here;" "You look hot with those boots, should we put the kid to bed and..."

There is scientific research on this too. **Couples who describe themselves as unhappily married notice only half of the positive interactions they have with their partners, compared to happily married couples who instead do notice the positive**. Unhappy partners focus on all the partner's mistakes and shortcomings.

Happy couples naturally – and some by effort – do notice and stow into memory kind acts or words or aspects of their partners. We should also stop and learn to acknowledge more, and voice our appreciation vocally for, our partner's good deeds. Even watching a positive movie clip predisposes us to be more understanding and compromising.

Once we have not only openly acknowledged but also stored to memory our partner's positive act, we can then reminisce about it when we are separated. Or even more importantly, when a disagreement surfaces. By having been exposed recently to a positive interaction, real or relived in our brain, our reaction to a new challenge will be so much more balanced, accepting, non-confrontational. It's scientifically proven.

We seek admiration from our partner perhaps because admiration is a tangible evidence of love. **We fall in love with the image our partner has of ourselves**. They see us as perfect, beautiful, smart, funny, etc. Our ego relishes the compliments and the adoration. When our partner does project our image back at us as negative, we ourselves fall out of love.

Be with someone who brings out the best in you[28]

What is best in me I owe to her.
Barack Obama

It is a gift to live your life with a person you love who is wiser than you.
Jerome Groopman, in 'How doctors think'

I love you not only for what you are, but for what I am when I am with you. I love you not only for what you have made of yourself, but for what you are making of me. I love you for the part of me that you bring out.
Elizabeth Barrett Browning

You should be of the firm belief that your partner makes you better, to be able to achieve love happiness long-term. Your partner should be perceived as the one who **makes you a person closer to the ideal of the person you are yearning to be.**

Be with someone who brings out the best in you. Our partner should be our best teacher, educator. The word **'education' comes from the Latin *e-ducare*, literally translated as 'to lead out of.'** So when we educate people, we should not stuff something into their minds; rather, we lead this something out of them; we **help them find what their own passions and strengths and fears are**, bringing the unconscious to awareness.

This point is a corollary to fostering each other's admiration, and extends it to the fact that appreciating our partner's points of view after understanding it deeply and truly should lead to **having our partner influence us.**

It's really beautiful to listen carefully and be able to understand our lover's point of you. **Even criticism towards ourselves should be seen calmly, and explored for true opportunities for us to grow.** Just

132

because we thought being a certain way was a good thing does not mean that instead that causes angst in our partner – as well as probably many others.

Partners are attracted by the good they see in the other person. That goodness in the partner makes them want to be a better person. **"You make me want to be a better man," is a sign the relationship is working**. We want to emulate the positive virtue the other possess, the virtue that we know makes our relationship better, and even the world better. A successful love relationship is about **two people gradually changing each other for the better**.

An example for my personality is that I've always believed that being openly happy was great for others too. That being propositive and always offering to do something – often sports and other outdoor activities – was great for all. Instead at times I've learned from friends and lovers that I can be too much for them. I have to learn that certain people I adore might not always jump at the opportunity for a soccer match or a long bike ride or a big party.

Feedback is a good thing. What we might like this moment, might not be exactly what our partner wants, and that we should understand. Be open to the fact that what sounds like criticism of what you have proposed or done might not be a personal attack on you, but an opportunity for you to grow and see the other side of things, another opinion.

Studies show that **men who allowed their wives to influence them, had happier relationships** and were less likely to eventually divorce than men who resisted their wives' influence.

We need to expand our own being by including our partner within ourselves. This **self-expansion to include our partner in our life, in our interests, in our emotions, sharing our thoughts and feeling**, is a catalysts for positive emotions.

When persons in a couple draw each of them as circles, the more the two circles overlap, the better the relationship is likely to fare. Two circles with no overlap means the two individuals lead separate lives, and do not share. The more overlap, the more the two lovers are open to letting the other into their lives, including the deepest emotions, most profound thoughts, with no secrets.

True sharing comes when you begin to feel your partner emotions after she shares her thoughts. In a positive relationship, we can pass along our feelings to our partners through an emotional contagion. First we share positive emotions with the partner. Then we synchronize behaviors and biochemistry with our partner. Finally we invest in each other well-being, as we know our happiness depends on the happiness of our partner. We want to help our partner grow and flourish, as we love the essential goodness of our partner's character.

We are **built to mimic each other**. As infants, we start mimicking our parents as soon as we are born. As adults, we tend to synchronize our facial expressions, vocalization, postures, and behaviors with those around us, and as a result eventually true bonding results in similar emotions. We catch both positive and negative emotions from people we closely interact with.

It's obviously as important for wives to get influenced by their husbands. Studies have shown that women already follow advice of the men in their lives. Women should absolutely do not get influenced too much by their male partners, as they would risk becoming depressed, which would be detrimental to their health and to the relationship.

Interestingly, other research shows that **the partners of men who accept their influence are far less likely to be harsh with their male counterparts**. A **willingness to share power and to respect the other's point of view is a prerequisite for compromising**. And there is much that women can teach men; for example, often, the value of friendship. And how to express and discuss feelings.

Studies show that **80% of the time, it's the woman who brings up sticky relationship issues, while the man avoids discussing them**. And this is true in both happy and unhappy relationships.

In studies, about **35% of men are emotionally intelligent**. Relationships that are good and last need more emotionally intelligent men. Emotionally intelligent husbands is the next step in social evolution. Husbands who put their wives and family first, and not their careers. Husbands who can accept their wives' influence, tend to be outstanding fathers, too.

Moreover, these dads are passing on their kids an understanding and respect for one's own emotions and those of others. They 'emotionally coach' their offspring. Not accepting influence, instead, will decrease the male's influence. **Often in life one needs to yield in order to win.**

So if your wife complains about the raised toilet seat, let her influence you, and put it back down after you are done peeing. A raised toilet seat is symbolic for male entitlement for many women.

Another classic example is **for one partner to want to keep the house sparkling clean, not considering the other's opinion** on what can be instead more important. Sometimes it might be preferable for the receiving partner to have a lover who is positive and open to cuddling and quality time, than to have a perfect house keeper.

One can pay a house keeper, and should not have to pay for a relaxed smiling partner. A male family member of mine does not have the perfect house in terms of tidiness, but does receive empathic love by his partner, who constantly hugs and kisses him. That's preferable for me to the contrary.

Your partner's **criticism should be viewed as having some basis in reality**. It should be viewed as a chance to have **not monocular, but binocular vision**. It should be perceived and received as a way to see the world in more than just your narrow point of view.

At the same time, we should not completely disappear in a relationship. Each person should be secure and mature within herself and himself. The partner should not compete with us, but complement us, make us even better.

In a relationship, we should strive to help our partner become what they want to be. We need to change with them, as they follow their dreams with our support. We should not become just what the other person needs from us, but as importantly what we strife to be.

When you start a relationship, you and your partner may have some rough edges, some idiosyncrasies, even some outright flaws. We all do. **As you stay together, you slowly wear down those rough edges**, until they become smooth, as you have reached a deep understanding of each other.

In long-term love happiness, staying with a partner means we still believe **our partner will continue to make us a better person**. We believe that our partner will **continue to make our life joyous, free, happy**. We continue to live in love happiness with our partner **when we see the future as bright, jolly, blissful**. We can't keep the flame alive just by memories, by gratitude.

Let your partner make the best in you come out. There must be belief that the influence of our partner will makes us a better person. We want to be a better person because of the love we feel from our partner. **We love our partner so much that we want to become the best possible partner they could ever dream for themselves**.

Sharing common important goals; creating shared meaning[28]

Happiness is only real when shared.

In my book on happiness,[1] we saw how having goals is one of the six keys to achieving personal happiness. Having shared goals is one of the crucial factors to achieving long-term love happiness. Not all these goals have to be huge, like eradicating world hunger.

For example, a goal can be to create rituals of connections. It's nice to share customs, like Sunday dinner with extended family. Or rituals, like a religious holiday celebration. Thanksgiving playing football.[30] More stories, like when partners first met, and their first trip together, can be purposely created.

Another important objective can be to support each other's roles. Shared meaning also means to speak candidly and respectfully to each other. Better communication creates a blending of your common sense of meaning. Create always new shared values and symbols.

Life gives us the opportunity to come up with so many **new projects together**. First the honeymoon, then the house, then the kids, then travel, then the beach house, then taking care of older parents, then serials on tv, movie nights, organizing parties with friends, cooking classes.

Life is a long journey; see and do something different with your loved one along the way. The famous Greek philosopher Heraclitus taught that "Panta rei," meaning "Everything flows," everything changes with time. Rejoice in the different opportunities you'll have along a lifespan to share common goals with your beloved partner.

Life in a successful love relationship should become more about 'we' than 'I'. Some 'I' will remain, such as, "I'll go out with friends once a month," or "I'll go play golf every 6 weeks for a day." But much of the relationship should be around the 'we', such as, "We'll go out to dinner once a week," "We'll share house chores," "We'll commit to spending at least an hour a day in quality relationship time."

One obvious example of a shared goal is **having kids**. Wanting kids, because **our partner is so wonderful we want to reproduce him**. Each partner is extraordinary to the eyes of the other, and so we want to make another extraordinary human being, with similar characteristics to our loved one.

Not all people want to have children. In fact, research shows that having children does not necessarily improve love happiness. Empathic love depends on other traits. So please discuss at the beginning with your partner what you main life goals are. If you long to have children, and your partner does not, that might be a non-starter.

Having kids should be a possible common goal, and not the sole goal of a love relationship. The survival of our species depends on kids ultimately outgrowing the initial family they were born in, venturing courageously into the world and eventually creating their own life and love relationships.

Kids are supposed over time to lose patience with their parents and grandparents, and seek their own path. For a parent, success means eventually being taken for granted, and letting go. At that point the parent will remain again alone with the partner, and will remain happy only if between the two of them there is solid love happiness.

Other examples of shared goals are volunteer work, environmental actions, a social issue, traveling, gardening, a sport, a tidy house, walking and hiking, buying a country house and making it homey, helping with grandkids, a religious experience, reading together, a tv series to have

137

common discussion on, going out camping, or even working quietly together in the same room on your own separate computers, and occasionally sharing thoughts and experiences.

The bedrock of a love relationship between two individuals is mutual respect for each other and a shared goal of becoming better individuals and working together to increase the goodness in the world. The relationship is rich in shared positive emotions and values.

The point is to spend time and have fun together.

<u>**Keeping the passion**</u>

Keeping a life together which is active, with always **new adventures, new common goals, with shared meaning**, is a key to ever-lasting empathic love. In passionate love, we are starting a new project of life together. Keeping some elements of passionate love means **finding ever new projects together**.

These could be a new house. A charity to work together. A new way to volunteer together. A new restaurant every week to have dinner together. A new theatre production. But also new ways to be physically and emotionally closely connected.

Men should continue to try and seduce their partner. Women should do the same. I love as my wife says that one should be more elegant and refined and sexy in their clothing at home than outside the home. Love needs to be continuously regenerated. Love may get sick over time, and then it will need a cure of more affection and cuddling and trust and complicity and sharing. Love needs to continually evolve.

Women love to receive flowers. To be wooed, to be seduced, to be wanted and supported. Men love to be complimented, to feel like they are special. It's vital to know what works for your partner, and continue to feed their needs forever, not just the first 3, or 5, or 10, or 20 years. FOREVER.

We need to keep lighted the reasons for why we fell in love. And we need to add along the years new reasons why that flame will continue burning bright and steady. Perhaps we'll discover that our partner can also be a great mother. And amazing volunteer. He'll learn to cook later in life. She'll get another degree, showing perseverance and love of learning and improving.

We'll realize that our partner is more than the unidimensional person we first met, when we noticed her amazing eyes, or his broad shoulders. She can be fragile. She can be strong willed. She can be dreamy. She can be focused. She can be wild. She can be conservative. She is, above all, dedicated to you. Dedicated to love. All in **one perfectly imperfect human being**.

Having common goals is a key to love happiness. Initially is shared feeling. Exchanging love languages. Then it could be helping the poor. Fighting discrimination. Denouncing racism. We need to **find newer revolutions to join to renew our love**. It could even be watching a series together and discussing its issues. Or taking care of old relatives.

Routine is an enemy of love. We may need some peace and quiet for short whiles, but in general most of us are looking for special new moments to enjoy. So experiencing something new together makes the love bond stronger. Learning together a new dimension of life is regenerating to our shared intimacy feelings. We add a new experience which connects us.

Each partner should strive to find new ways to strengthen the bond. One may be that one partner proposes new recipes. Another one that the other partner proposes new trips in nearby attractions. **Life should be a continuous discovery. A continuous amazement at the beauty that the world is. Each partner should share this joy of new wonders to explore with the other**.

Some may like new sexual experiences. Some new ways to interact with grandkids. Some exploring psychedelics together. Some joining a band or a choir. Tenderness is so important, and so undervalued. Again, human warmth is clean energy: so so true.

I love how some cultures do try to suggest acts to maintain the passion. When I was in the deep Sahara in Central Algeria, I saw women wearing a whole-body white drape from which only one eye was visible. I also saw shops with the most sexy, body-hugging, sparkling clothes, covering barely 20% of a woman's body. These Algerian women are super-sexy at home, to keep the passion alive for their husbands.

This is an extreme, and I think women should be free inside and outside the home, and equal to men. I do think, like I mentioned before, that **to be sexier-looking at home - for both men and women - than outside would keep more couples happy**. Too many men wear ridiculous slippers and stained torn-apart t-shirts with lousy underwear while at home.

We need to **make the extraordinary more common**. Read the book *Moments*,[31] which shows how we truly enjoy as human beings the times in life which take our breath away. They cannot happen every hour. But they can occur more than once every few years.

Millions of 80 year-old people are having sex as you read these lines. Why them yes, and not you? With good preliminaries, caressing, sweet talk, and true intimacy, or if needed, gel, women can be ready for intercourse and more. Men actually have less premature ejaculation and longer erections after 60 years of age.

Love making can actually be more satisfactory later in life than when we are in our 20's and inexperienced, naïve, unaware of our erogenous zones, quick to ejaculation, and unaware of how to best achieve a vaginal or a clitoridean orgasm.

Divorce commonly occurs when one partner loses hope that life will ever be again extraordinary. Couples separate when she sees in her partner no interest in rekindling aspects of passionate love. Any of them. When boring days watching tv or being on social media are all one can look forward to. This feels similar to being dead already. It's biologic survival, not purposeful living.

Life instead is action. Life demands ever new adventures. New discoveries together. We want to be reborn once in a while. We want to rediscover. To renew. To revisit. To renovate ourselves. To continuously improve and even notice ourselves and our partner under new facets. To relive another first day.

We are like babies who want to be independent but cannot do without our mother's hugs and kisses. We may have for a bit our mind in our work, but in the evening, **doing something fun with our partner is what we are living for.**

Passivity is the murderer of love. Inactivity from one partner, can kill the love of the other. Having a dictatorship of 'the same old' will eventually lead either to revolution – the other partner flees, or to death – the other partner stays but is not living really, is amorphous.

Keeping the passion is continuing to be caring, empathic, cuddly, physically and emotionally close towards each other, in ever new ways. We need to be able to keep the dream of love even after it has become reality. Being grateful for the past, and gung-ho for the future.

Solving your solvable problems[28]

None of us humans is perfect. Therefore perfection in a love relationship is a myth we should avoid. **Each couple, even the happiest one, has problems.** This is actually reassuring for all of us! It's important to face the difficulties, and to try to solve them smartly and amiably.

The **#1 problem reported by couples is balancing job and family.** The **#2 is the frequency of sex.** These are solvable problems, if we raise awareness about them with our partner, and openly and actively look for mutually-agreeable solutions.

Try to really understand your partner's point of you. Forget your view for a few moments. Truly put yourself in your partner's shoes while listening intently to what she says. Then communicate, with empathic love, that you see the issue from her perspective.

Start your feedback softly. Treat your partner with respect. Resist bursting back with raised voices and full neck veins. Relax. There should be no criticism, contempt, defensiveness, or stonewalling. Share accountability for the issue. **Share how you feel. And what you need.**

Make statements that start with "I" instead of "you". Better to say, "I would like if you listened to me for 2 minutes," than "You are not listening to me."

If there is an **enduring vulnerability** that makes you feel a particular way, make sure you share it. Your partner should understand the reason why you have particular triggers. May be you need to share something from your childhood. Or from a past relationship. Do not keep major secrets which hold the key to your feelings.

One trick to effective communication is **any statement or action – even silly – that tries to prevent the sparkle of negativity to spin out of control**. Some have called these **repair attempts**.[28] Repair attempts try to de-escalate conflict, with phrases like, "Let's take a break," "Wait, I need to calm down," "May be we should go and get some fresh air now," "Perhaps you wanted to say that in a different way," etc.

Without de-escalating moments, a provocation can lead to flooding, i.e. being overwhelmed in the fight and losing control, mounting to personal attacks to each other's character, name calling, and worse.

Learn to make and receive repair attempts. For example, **take some responsibility** for the problem, **"I know this is not all your fault. I know I play a role in this issue as well."** It's also important to listen carefully. Sometimes the repair attempt may be not well delivered, e.g. with a harsh tone of voice, but it is still an invitation to truce, e.g. "Can we take a break?"

Appreciate a "sorry". **Saying you are sorry can be magical in a relationship**. Tell your partner what you are apologizing for. Be specific about your regrets. And share what you see are your negative contributions to the conflict.

Accept the repair attempt. View the interruption as a bid to make things better. **The break should be at least 20 minutes if there has been a heated argument. It takes that long for your heart beat to slow down**, and for hormones and adrenaline to readjust to near baseline. Research shows that **if your heart beat exceeds 100, you are not able to hear what your spouse is trying to tell you**, no matter how hard you try.

Compromise. A soft start up, giving and accepting repair attempts, and keeping calm, allows the couple to be able to negotiate successfully. There is no compromise without you being willing to accept to be influenced in some way by your partner. You have to be open to at least considering her opinion. Sadly, research shows that men have a harder time accepting influence from their wives than vice versa.

An example of how to solve problems with some acceptance and some compromise, is to simply state, "I want you to accept that I am more emotional than you, and need more time to talk things through with you, one on one. It is not a flaw of mine. I just need you to understand this, and accept me as I am, being willing to listen more next time."

A common issue in couples is that one earns more, and expects the other to do more house work. This used to be true for most of history, with the man gathering food, or more recently salary from his work, and the woman caring to the kids and the house. Thankfully that's not true anymore.

Women now often work and earn outside the house more than men. These women should not do more housework, and more kids tasks. There should be an open dialogue clarifying each partner's role. I know many men who are happily 'not working,' and who take care of the house and the kids. There are many in my own block here in Philadelphia, USA.

It is refreshing that each partner can have a choice of how to best use her/his talents, and a negotiation cooperatively develops on how to split duties and tasks. Remember the Aikido principle of yielding to win. The more you are able to make concessions, the better able you'll be to persuade your spouse.

Process any grievances so they do not linger. Solve the conflict as soon as possible. **Do *not* go to sleep with the wound still open.**

Typical solvable problems are **work stress. In-laws. Money. Sex. Housework. Internet distractions. A new baby.** These are the most typical areas of marital conflict.

Stress: Unwind, relax, exercise, meditate, make sure you have some time to take your mind off things somehow.

In-laws: The worst relationship is often between wife and mother-in-law. **The husband needs to take decisively the side of his wife.** The couple needs to establish 'we-ness' above all else, including a mother or a father or a sibling. Long-term empathic love can only start when we-ness includes **when the man lets his mother know that his partner is now first in his heart**. This may feel difficult, but it is so crucial and absolute.

Money: Studies show that about $100,000 per couple is often what is needed for economic serenity currently. If you make less, or spend more, you may need to itemize, keeping track of expenditures. And you need to budget, keeping weekly/monthly updates on finances. Plan your financial future.

Housework: The solutions here are, 1. Hire more help; 2. Men do more work in the house. Men should do well to be more helpful domestically: women find a man's willingness to do housework extremely erotic, research has shown. Divide and conquer house tasks, according to preferences.

A new baby: I was so surprised when, researching evidence for my happiness book,[1] I discovered that having kids does not improve relationships. For a woman, becoming a mother causes a seismic change in the meaning of her life. All of a sudden, a defenseless human depends mostly just on her.

For the man, instead, the fear is to lose his wife to the new baby. The only choice is to join her head-on into the new world she has entered with such passion. Without jealousy, but instead with the same love towards a common goal, the baby's well-being.

At 3 months, the baby will begin to smile, and bring such joy to both parents, if they are willing to see things positively, as they should. **The mother should continue to care about the male partner's needs, and vice versa.**

Sex: This is a big area of potential embarrassment, hurt, and rejection. Good sex depends mostly on how well the couple is doing emotionally. In particular, sex is directly correlated to a women's mental happiness in the relationship. Research has shown, for example, that women have more orgasms when couples are able to talk comfortably about this topic.

The goal of sex in a long-term rapport is to have fun, heightened closeness, and feel valued and accepted in this tender area of the relationship. Experts say that 10-15% of a relationships should be good sex. My mother said always, "Over 50%!" Enjoy it while you can, on both sides.

Be able to compromise at times. A chef does not get mad when a customer is not in the mood for pasta tonight, but instead wants salmon. Make sure you as a partner satisfy what your partner is in the mood for. Make sure your partner knows what you like. Discover in detail what she likes, what brings her pleasure. Talk about sexual intimacy openly. You are not an immature teenager anymore.

Learn how to initiate sex in a way your partner likes. And learn how to refute – if you have to – sex gently. The more you can hear, understand, and respect your partner's occasional 'no', the more 'yes' there will be later, if there is sincerity and openness on both sides.

Old wounds that may still be lingering. The only way out is to confront them, accept them, change, or find some other compromise, a final solution. The sooner, the better. **Issues left unspoken and unresolved will erode the relationship**.

Accepting your partner: I love you despite

And most importantly of all,
I will love you unconditionally.
I will love you
Simply for being you.
Joel Delizo

Real love, I've learned, is a very, very strong form of forgiveness. I do not think people yearn for love because they hate staying home alone on Saturday night or because they dread going into restaurants alone. People want love because they want their taped-together glasses or ten extra pounds to be forgiven. They want someone to look past the surface stuff like bad-hair days, a too-loud laugh or potato chips crunching in the living-room couch when anyone sits down.

Lois Smith Brady

Love comes when you stop demanding from your partner what she cannot give you. Love the other the way they want to be loved. **Accept the other as she is. Do not try to change them!!**

Women, and men, usually want a partner who loves them for who they are. A partner with passion as an eternal lover. And a partner they can trust like their dad (for women), or mom (for men). This is perhaps the number one error I see people do. They commit long-term during passionate love, hoping their love to they partner will change the partner. Wrong!!

First, identify the core problem. These are often related to responsibilities (e.g. laundry, kids, etc), and intimacy (e.g. physical touch, cuddling, sex, etc). I am late because of traffic. You are late because you are inconsiderate. Is it a one-time issue? Or a pattern? Can you accept it if it's a pattern? We certainly cannot force change through personal vile attacks to our partner's own personality. It will only enrage and/or discourage our loved one.

Second, do the DEEP analysis.[32] **D stands for Differences** in personality and interests that might contribute to conflict. **E stands for Emotional sensitivities** that may make the differences more difficult to handle. The second **E stands for External stressors** that might complicate the resolution of the conflict. **P stands for patterns of communication.**

A relationship conflict can be resolved either through acceptance or change. And there is also **a third way. A combination of acceptance and change**. Acceptance by one partner and change by the other. A compromise. This is often the best solution.

Acceptance means tolerating what you regard as an unpleasant behavior of your partner. It also means you somehow understand that behavior, and you bear with it because you have comprehended it in a deeper meaning, and perhaps even appreciate its value and importance in the relationship.

Acceptance in this case does not mean submission. Submission comes from weakness. Acceptance comes from a position of strength. You tolerate the aversive behavior because you yourself have chosen to tolerate it, as you see it in a broader contest, part of the many properties of your partner. You could fight it, but you consciously decide not to.

An example could be a partner who nags the other about too much work. You might like your work, get a lot of satisfaction from it, and a complaining partner is unpleasant. But you chose to tolerate it as you see it as your partner's cry for you to spend more time with him, more time with the family, more time together.

Acceptance is the best starting place, for most problems. If we are the one who is to accept the other's 'flaw,' **the best way to start the process of acceptance is by understanding**. To understand is to forgive, and to accept. Because we do not like what our partner does, does not mean he does it on purpose.

Understanding the root of the behavior is key. And the understanding must be both ways. The person 'committing' the unpleasant behavior for the other, must explain why he is behaving a certain way. A parent did the same thing? They have some bowel disease that makes them fart? Are they allergic to pollen and that's why they hate traveling?

And the person 'receiving' the unwanted behavior must explain what particular emotion is triggered by the partner's behavior: does it remind herself of the inability by her father of spending quality time with her mother, which ruined that relationship, and makes her feel gloom and doom all over again when it happens in her own relationship?

Understanding emotional sensitivities and external stressors is so important in handling conflict in the most positive way possible.

When you are upset, try to reveal your emotional state to your partner without blaming her for it. Explain what you are feeling, and why. Expressing soft emotions such as hurt and sorrow may actually bring our partner closer. Voicing that you feel lonely, disappointed, neglected, can trigger caring and concern from your partner. Use 'I' statements, describing how you feel and what you want. Do not use in general 'you' statements, attacking your partner directly. Do not accuse the other.

When your partner is upset, try to understand and ask about her emotional state. Inquire about why she feels so strongly about this issue. Acknowledge the feeling of your partner without blame or judgement.

147

Initially, do not share your own upset, but just share how you understand now what the distressed partner is feeling. Our partner side of the story is really important for you to make your own; walk in your partner's shoes before sharing how it feels to walk into your own shoes.

Understanding derives from open communication devoid of secrets. **Effective understanding comes disclosing to our partner what we have never disclosed to anyone else**. Are your emotions linked to the way you were raised, by somethings your parents did? By what you experienced with a previous lover?

Much unhappiness comes into the world because of things left unsaid, Dostoyevsky wrote. What we don't want to say, and don't say, is more important than what we say. You need to share to your partner hidden emotions and the cause of those emotions. Sharing these sensitivities will bring you closer; you'll change because by sharing you change and improve; **your partner listens and better understands**, which leads to some acceptance.

Mindfulness is in-the-moment attention to what is happening, and must be applied to love relationships. We must have a non-judgmental awareness of our feelings, our partner's feelings, and how we are interacting, in particular regarding communication. Each discussion, each conflict, should aim for mindfulness.

Looking at this from the point of view of the partner with the 'flaw,' feeling that our partner loves us the way we are, flaw and all, is inestimable. We do not have to deny who we are. We know we inherited from our father being a bit messy. It's gratifying that our partner can accept us the messy way we are. We do not have to deny ourselves. "**I love you just the way you are**" is one of the most wonderful phrases we can hear from our loved one.

Perhaps we love trashy love novels, or tv shows. It's refreshing that our partners lets us read them, or watch them, without shaming us. We feel safe, relaxed, because our partner is the only one who lets us be ourselves. We do not have to hide aspects of our person. Even an occasional fart is pardoned. We are finally safe and nurtured. We have reached a nice place to be, a comfortable safe harbor. The journey becomes more effortless, more truthful, more honest, more spontaneous.

Interestingly, science shows that partners commonly restructure their initial expectations to more closely fit with the reality of their partner, perceive their partner to more closely resemble their ideal than they actually do, and enhance negative partner qualities by associating unfavorable attributes with more virtuous traits.[33] Positive couples have partners who try to accept each other's flaws.

Compared to acceptance, **change is more difficult**, and is usually **self-directed. One changes because he wants to, because he feels things will be better by changing**. And one changes more easily if the partner requests the change with a direct, positive request, such as, "I would love for you to split the laundry duty with me, so I do it on Wednesday, and you do it on Sunday." What is much more difficult to change is the 'want.'

We would love our partner to not only 'do the do,' e.g. do the laundry on Sunday, but also 'want the do,' e.g. *want* to do the laundry on Sunday. **Changing desires and emotions is a lot more difficult**. Here the acceptance should come in understanding that **behavior change was hard enough, and desire change may be sometimes too much to ask**.

The **silver bullet of change is that you should first change yourself**. You have direct control over your behavior. Changing yourself first in order to change the relationship is the #1 key to positive change.

Rather than complaint and criticize, take constructive action. Do not curse the darkness, and be unwilling to just light a candle or switch on the light. Do something positive for your partner, with no strings attached. Do not necessarily expect positive actions from your partner in response to your positive action. Do what your partner has been asking you to do.

Even avoidant people can work on strategies to change and stop pushing love away. But they cannot be forced. They need to want to change themselves, if they truly want love happiness the way it's scientifically proven to happen.

First, they need to **learn to identify deactivating strategies, like constant criticizing, and avoid them**. Second, they should de-emphasize self-reliance and focus instead on mutual support.

Third, they can find a secure partner, who can make them more secure in their attachment. Fourth, they can work on being aware of their tendency to misinterpret in a negative way their partner's behaviors. Fifth, focus, write down, and notice positive behaviors in your partner.

One cannot and should not change the core aspects of their partner. You chose them the way they are. Idiosyncrasies and all. You have accepted your partner by entering into the relationship. **People cannot alter what is at their core.** A giraffe has a long neck, and can't change it. You cannot ask your partner to change who he is.

In fact, psychology calls these tries to change the partner 'regulatory attempts,' and associate them with a lowering of the receiving partner's self-esteem. Telling someone they have a flaw, means in some way you do not like who they are.[33]

Each of us may have pre-relationship 'ideal standards,' and we might be quick to criticize our partner when we see the partner does not meet that standard. Sadly, studies show that partner's judgments play a more powerful role in predicting relationship satisfaction than self-judgements.[33]

Partners can change what is at their character's periphery. While we cannot change much from being introvert to extrovert, from being a spender to a saver, we can change, for example, our pattern of communication. Once we have identified the areas of conflict, what we can change is how we discuss them, how we communicate about them. Both partners can learn to be less defensive, and better listeners of the other's point of view and preferences.

Neither change nor acceptance nor compromise is easy. But we should make them common. Because if we do not resolve the conflict with either of these solutions, the issue will erode our love relationship.

The **pattern of communication** is key. Perhaps most important is to choose our words carefully. We should not say, "You are frigid," but rather, "I have this feeling of rejection and unlove when you decline to cuddle with me." We need to talk about the 'it,' the fact. We do not have to attack the 'you,' the whole being of our partner.

Eventually, if you truly have shared emotions, and background secrets, and have listened carefully to the other side, being open to both some change and some understanding, the mutual feeling of renewed, in fact more profound, bonding, will benefit the relationship. Confiding feelings and hidden emotions can lead to greater intimacy, as we feel closer to our partner now. Conflict can be resolved positively, often using languages of love such as physical touch, gifts, quality time, words of affirmation and acts of kindness.

Forgiveness is key to long term love happiness success. Letting go of resentment and absolving a person's bad conduct is often the right and good thing to do.

In a successful long-term relationships, what begins to be cherished the most are actually the idiosyncrasies, the things that in the past we saw as possible flaws. **Robin Williams, in Good Will Hunting, misses the most, of his wife who died a few years earlier, the fact she would pass gas in her sleep.** That's true empathic love.

Willingness to give something up

Later in passionate love, we begin to **test our lover**. We have them go through truth quizzes. Is their story consistent? What do other say about them? Most importantly, we begin to have each other go through **tests of reciprocity**. A common project begins to be developed, and each may **need to give up something**.

We ask our partner to agree to our part of the project. "Do you love me?" in these circumstances means, "Do you accept to be part of the project which I proposed?" When the partner answers, "I love you," that means the partner is agreeing to the project, is moving willingly towards the preference of the proposing partner.

Asking, "Do you love me?" in these conversations means "Will you change? How will you change? Are you willing to come to my side?" So "Do you love me?" is a request for the partner to give up something. To do something the asking partner wants. There are many examples.

One instance is when a partner keeps his lover separated from his work. When he never asks her to come on a trip. He wants to keep her separated from some part of his life. In this circumstance, for her to discuss this issue, and during it asking, **"Do you love me?"**, is not just a

151

request to answer, "Yes, of course, I love you!" It's **a call for him to take her on some work trips**, for him to make her a bigger part of his work life.

Empathic true love cannot be achieved without *both* partners each giving up something.

In fact, at times it seems that each partner makes huge demands to the other. "You cannot live with you mother, we will live together with nobody else." "You cannot go out with friends as much as before." "You cannot spend as much times at work as before." "You'll have to golf once a week, not 3 times a week." "You'll have to have sex only with me for the rest of your life."

It might feel at times like the partner demands are aimed at destroying the other. The asked partner might feel like these changes will make him be another person all together, possibly more removed from his true self. It might feel even like losing one's own soul, certainly like losing so many habits, traditions.

What do you mean Christmas with your family, alternating with mine? Vacationing without my best friend? No beer night with my college buddies? 'Behaving' during a bachelor party? This seems just too much to accept.

Love requests have forever seemed unreasonable. **God asked Abraham to prove his love by killing his own first son, Isaac**. Love seems absurd in his demands. The reciprocity test is a battle in which each partner asks the other to surrender a little, sometimes a lot. To give up often something that before the partner receiving the demand thought indispensable for her survival.

Each of us wants to be loved through asking seemingly impossible tasks to the new lover. Other common illustrations are, "You have to move to my city," "You should probably change job and make more money," "You cannot live anymore so close to your folks, I can't stand their frequent invasions."

So one ends up bargaining that if one moves to the city where the partner goes, he is allowed to be supported financially by the other. Or if one wants kids badly and the other less, the one who wants kids takes more responsibility in their upbringing and costs. And so on.

Eventually, like in any negotiations, demands may not be agreed on. Any negotiation has limits which are unacceptable to one member. There is a hard end that cannot be passed. At that point, a **mutually agreed pact** develops. The partner asked to do something has given all she can; the partner asking **must accept this limit**.

We **should not demand to change the partner excessively**. Let's make the example of the man who gets attracted to a younger woman because she is carefree, loves to party, is social. Demanding she gets completed 'domesticated,' stays at home most of the day, does not party anymore, becomes an housewife who just takes care of the kids, shopping, cleaning, and cooking, **destroys the very person he fell in love with**.

Some major character trait which attracted us during passionate love should not be destroyed over time by empathic love. In fact these characteristics should be worshipped, enhanced, cultivated. Making the extraordinary person a daily ground-hog-day boring individual is what often kills relationships.

So **love eventually rests on this mutually agreed pact**. Love gets a bit **institutionalized**. Gets its rules and deals. A contract which fits both, even if both have given up something, so to gain something bigger.

This is a point so important to understand. **Every time we change something, we gain something, and we also lose something**. I moved to the USA when I was 19 and gained tremendous personal and professional opportunities; and gave up time with my parents and siblings. Some compromises are so hard; but we must choose.

One changes job, and gives up the perks of the old employment. One gives up singlehood for couplehood, and loses some freedom. One goes to the movies, and cannot go out to a restaurant with other friends. It's inescapable. You can't have it both ways.

Men and women could continually look for a better partner. Some are addicted to the fact that the grass may be greener on the other side. Some are addicted to passionate love, and never learn empathic love.

For myself, I find that **when I'm in true love happiness** with my partner, as I am now for many years with my wife, **I am not attracted to other women**. I don't dream about conquering them. I am quiet delighted that my emotional and physical needs are already in good hands, those of my partner, and my hormonal milieu does not point me at all to stray away from outside the paradisiacal nest I already live in. **Reflect that many times what you are giving up, you actually do not want anymore!**

The important attitude is to be aware that to put more tea in our cup, some old tea must fist come out. A new tea develops. A new reality. That, assuming we were the ones making the choice of transformation, should fit us overall better, and make us happier. We can't move to college as a growing experience, and then miss our parents every single hour. We made a conscious choice. We must stick by it, especially psychologically.

I have seen people move from one continent to another, away from original family and friends, away from a great job and a wonderful apartment, for love. Bargaining the certain for the uncertain but potentially overall better. Only people with this courageous attitude have a chance of getting to eventual empathic, satisfying love.

Some studies show that **love that is born from a bigger revolution, it's often deeper and more truthful. When both sides have to revolutionize their lives, then love has a bigger chance to last and be wonderful.** Once a couple with him German and her Thai, of completely different cultures, religions, and languages, told me they had to love each other more than other couples. And they seemed genuinely happy in love after over 35 years.

People who have to give up little, or nothing, have often less intense, more superficial love. Love of people who went to war to love each other is more profound. Obviously this love is more difficult, may need to go through a longer path, and may have a higher chance of initial failure, but when it works, it's the emblem of empathic love.

Having reasonable expectations of love

When one is in love, one always begins by deceiving oneself, and one always ends up deceiving others. That is what the world calls romance.
Oscar Wilde

One cannot pretend to find everything they are dreaming of – e.g. looks, courage, wealth, humor, positivity, life-style, etc – **all in one person**. It's best to decide which one – or 2 or 3 maximum – trait is most important – e.g. honesty; sincerity, etc. One trait that is indispensable. Pick from table 6, for example.

To want everything is a recipe for disaster, unhappiness. Finding love is an adventure that **mixes dreams with realism**; this is where love happiness is found.

Do not expect perfection in your partner. As you enter the period past passionate and into empathic love, you'll discover more virtues, but also some characteristics that to you are flaws. **Everyone is always impossible at some time to live with, for you.** Your partner is the one you have chosen to accept despite the flaws.

The 'romantic' idea of **finding the perfect partner is a recipe for love unhappiness**. One is ready for long-term love when the idea of perfection is abandoned. **We can only claim to know our partner well when they have disappointed us, as we have identified a substantial flaw**. The chances of you being the exception and finding someone with no flaws are non-existent!

A recipe for not finding empathic love is believing in old stereotypes that history and media pass along to us. **For women, the attraction to power, money**, the hope for nice clothes, nice cars, nice houses. Models marry the rich, the rich marry models. Most of the times, these relationships do not work, as they are not based on the principles we describe in this book.

Equally doomed is the **attraction by men for beautiful women**. Beauty, as we know, goes away with age. And even when present, is so much less important that the values in Table 6, and 7. It's so refreshing that women now have a lot more power than 50, 100 years ago. And some men end up being the 'beauty' and some women the 'power.' Still, such combinations are hard to sustain over time unless better values (Table 6) are present.

Perhaps my favorite movie ever is, 'Some like it hot.' Marilyn Monroe is a beautiful but poor musician. Jack Lemmon with Tony Curtis's help, changes persona from a poor musician to a rich yacht-owning oil millionaire (this was 1956) to attract Marilyn, which works perfectly as they get together finally at the end of the movie. **What 'romantic' movies do not show 99% of the times, is life after the initial agreement to start the romantic relationship.**

Beautiful women need money to maintain their beauty, with hairdressers, personal trainers, stylists, make-up specialists, even at times plastic surgeons. And rich men probably need beautiful women to boost their own ego, for themselves and for everyone to see and envy. But this is ephemeral.

After looking at the evidence for what works, I can honestly and strongly recommend that **to find long-term empathic love women don't need to enhance their looks, and men do not need to fatten their pocket book.**

That is why it is **crucial to get to know first yourself,** and then the options out there. Date a bunch before committing forever. It helps to have a few lovers before settling down. This way you can experience directly that indeed there is no perfect match, no 'one-in-a-million' unique individual made just for you.

By experiencing different people, you can best decide what fits you best. What qualities are most important and truly not compromisable. This way you can decide which flaws you might be ok to live with. Because there will be flaws. Everyone will be a bit wrong for you when you get to know them well. So it's important to focus on the good, on the positive.

Long-term love somehow comes down to identifying **which variety of suffering we would most like to sacrifice ourselves for**. We have surveyed the different options for flaws, and we have identified and decided which ones are quite acceptable, given the virtues in our partner we greatly benefit from.

The partner who is best suited for us is also the one who can negotiate the inevitable differences with maturity, honest communication, intelligence and good grace. When you see that your partner is capable of understanding your craziness, your faults, your imperfections, then you should pause and enjoy the possibility of true long-term bliss.

And in response, please be aware that you'll never get to empathic, long-term love without embracing your partner's imperfections. A good long-term love relationship requires commitment, discipline, the courage to change and grow. Love happiness is hard work.

Think for a moment about living with your best friend for a long time. Even with her, life eventually would become difficult. Or think about living with your favorite parent. **Even your idolized relative will eventually drive you crazy.** The very people who make us the happiest, can make us also unhappy at times.

After all, my great friend Tonino does make fun of me at times. Antonello even more. I love them for that. But probably I would get angry at these behaviors if we lived together for a long time. So if we would suffer even living with our best friend, why would we expect not to struggle a bit with our partner at times?

Being able to admit that we will never completely satisfy our partner, and that we will never feel like our partner completely satisfy us, is liberating, eye-opening. Nobody else can be everything we have dreamed of; but our partner comes pretty close, and that is enough.

Productive fighting

Quarrels are the dowry that partners in a long-term love relationship bring one another.
                                        Ovid

Another element associated with healthy, long-lasting relationship is **how partners fight.** It's actually **healthy to see things differently, and express our disagreements.** But there are ways to resolve conflict associated with emotional success.

First, the partner should show concern for the other's well-being. There should be communication that the other's mental safety is at least as important as your own. In fact, our happiness is dependent on our partner's happiness – and vice versa. This whole book has emphasized this basic principle of dependency.

Second, the focus should be on the matter at hand. One trick is to **discover the 'dream' behind the conflict.** Say for example, one partner really wants to have dinner out on Sunday night. The other wants to relax at home. It's helpful for the partner who wants to dine out to share that she did that with her family, and she thought it was a lovely tradition she wants to continue.

It's important to **become a dream detective**. What is really the reason behind the standoff attitude? Acknowledging and respecting each other's deepest, most personal hopes and thoughts is key to saving and enriching your relationships.

Third, the couple should **refrain from generalizing** the disagreement. A partner should not bring up issues with the extended family of the partner when she wants to continue a tradition such as dinner out. Keep it to the issue. Do not generalize, and do not bring in old issues.

Fourth, there should be **willingness on both sides to engage in conversation**, without grandstanding and without stonewalling. In fact, people should have a mindset to **expect their partner to have the best intentions**, and mean the best for the relationship.

Fifth, and perhaps most important, **the true, underlying reason for our stance should be communicated effectively, including how we feel**. You cannot expect your partner to read your mind, even if you have been together for years. If you have not told him, he does not know!

Finally, I would add to use **the pool of common meaning** concept. While there may be disagreement on the specific issue, there is agreement on putting the couple first, the family second, and on focusing on issues of intimacy and trust and respect, for example. Do not forget to voice the many issues you agree with, while discussing one you disagree on.

Power should be balanced in the couple to achieve long-term empathic love. Nobody is right. Often there is no absolute truth or reality in partners' conflicts. **There is no immaculate perception**, just two ways to see things. **Acceptance of our partner's stance is crucial**. And this should be communicated: "I accept your point of view," even if you do not agree with it.

Conflicts in fact can be divided in those that can be somewhat resolved, and in those who cannot, and are forever. It's important to understand the distinction. As 69% of marital problems are **perpetual**, it's important to let go on these and **agree to disagree**. In fact, learning to

158

keep these differences in check, and to perhaps treat them with true sincere humor, is the best way to move forward positively.

Sadly, **some of us have never learned how to discuss issues**, how to communicate during a disagreement. My parents, for example, did not pass those skills to me: my father would dictate the rule of law, and my mother would always accept it and back it up, at least publicly in front of us kids. The negotiations she tried were never public, and mostly unsuccessful. These skills should be taught in school and in each family, instead.

You cannot solve all your relationship conflicts, and you should embrace having some that will never be solved, without exploding every time the same old issue comes up. We also need to learn to accept some differences of opinions with our partner, and put them in a parking lot we should forget about.

It's key in a happy love relationship to **overcome gridlock**.[23] You need to be able to keep the perpetual problem from overwhelming your life. I always say to **worry and fight what you can change** to something more positive. **You should not waist time trying to change something that cannot be changed**.

Identify these areas of conflicts. Discuss them until no further data or feelings need to shared. And if disagreement persists, and can be managed, agree to disagree and laugh about it, putting the issue in the relationship perpetual problems, making an effort to be conscious not to argue about it anymore, agreeing to disagree in a mature and wise manner.

At the end of the argument, go back and focus on areas of agreement, and on reciprocal fondness and admiration. Enjoy the vast pool of common goals and agreements. Learn to view your partner's shortcomings and oddities as amusing parts of an overall awesome package.

Early (or late) signs of failure

Odi et amo. Quare id faciam, fortasse requiris. Nescio, sed fieri sentio et excrucior.
[From Latin: 'I hate and I love. Perhaps you'd ask why I do it. I don't know, but I feel that's what happens and I get tormented by it.']
                                                                    Catullus

Poor communication

No one person deserves your tears, and who deserves them surely won't make you cry.

                                                    Gabriel García Márquez

Being able to have positive conversations is one of the keys to a happy long-term love relationship. The incapacity to do so is one of the major red flags for failure to be happy in love. Some inability to stay cool while communicating is innate (Table 9).

Be attentive to early warnings of poor communication. Levels of the **stress hormone** adrenaline are 34% higher, and ACTH levels double, in couples who ended unhappy or divorced **while arguing as newlyweds** compared to couples who stayed happily married.[28]

People communicate in different styles. One partner may be more aggressive, and may raise his voice occasionally. The other partner may be more gentle and soft spoken. The importance is to share thoughts and fears. Every day. And listen. And discover the true reason beyond the issue raised.

An inability to communicate effectively is **marked by poor listening, and by no real willingness to accept, change, or compromise**. It gets couples to the horrible place of bad feelings and endless conflicts. There is no win-win pact possible. **It's my win, and your loss**.

One partner believes the other is just plain wrong, selfish. The partners begin to both feel like, "He does not care about my view. He is

160

not listening. He does not care how I feel. All that matters to him is getting his way, like always."

A related issue is that of **refusing to get intimate, especially in terms of sharing one's soul**. People are afraid of mental intimacy. For whatever prior experiences, or innate predisposition, or both, they do not feel like sharing their inner most thoughts, emotions, secrets. That is deadly for a true positive love happiness relationship.

While win-win expands the possibilities, a win-lose situation is a zero-sum game, with **one partner's victory bringing on the other partner's defeat and gloom**. And the win of the one partner is ephemeral as the other partner's misery will eventually destroy the winning partner too.

Poor communication often involves a **harsh** start up. Research shows that **one can tell 96% of the time how a 15-minute conversation will end, positively or negatively, by the tone and words used in the first three minutes.**[28] When a discussion starts with criticism, or sarcasm, it inevitably ends on a negative note, despite attempts to be nice. One cannot lead in an exchange with, "You are just so sloppy and careless," and then hope in a good outcome.

As we have seen, the beginning of love, passionate love, should be a blessed time, in which flaws of our partner are not apparent yet, and everything is magic. Some relationships begin right away with one partner disrespecting the other, being mean, abusive. This is seldom good.

Especially ominous it's when early arguments do not focus on the issue, but expand to fault the partner's character. So, if one loses a wallet, the partner reaction is not, "So sorry, it happens, I'm sure you were distracted by your work problems, this occurred to me too," but instead he goes into a personal attack, "You are just so careless. You are disorganized, removed from reality, just a mess, how did you survive so far?"

A second characteristic of poor communication involves **personal criticism, instead of a situational complaint**. Complaints focus your feedback on the specific event. "I am surprised. You had promised to make dinner tonight, and it's not ready. I love it when you have dinner ready as I get back from a long day at work," said in a moderate tone of voice.

Criticism is instead, "You just don't care about us, dinner is not ready again! You are worthless," with a venom tone.

A complaint focuses on: 1. How I feel; 2: The specific situation; 3. Here is what I would like. **A criticism attacks not the event, but the partner's character**. Often criticisms are accompanied by the words 'always' or 'never.' **"What's wrong with you?"** is a favorite of partner's darting criticisms to the core of the other partner's self.

Why does criticism start anyway? First, because the partner is unresponsive, and driving us crazy. The second source, comes from our own self-doubt. It is self-doubt that probably has developed over the course of one's life, particularly during childhood. In other words, it is criticism of oneself.

Criticism is toxic to a relationship, and sets off the deep-seated fear that we will be rejected and abandoned. It distances two soul like nothing else.

Complaints instead should be viewed positively. None of us is perfect. I for sure may leave a t-shirt in the wrong place at times. When my partner reminds me the t-shirt would be better in the walking-closet place for it, it triggers in my brain that my partner loves me, as she knows I do like neatness too. But she does not make the issue a personal attack on me.

A further third characteristic of poor communication is **contempt**. Contempt arises as a form of **superiority over one's partner**. It is a form of disrespect. **Name-calling, eye-rolling, mockery, and hostility** are all forms of contempt. Contempt is terrible in a relationship because it conveys **disgust** instead of compassionate empathic care.

"Go f* yourself," "You are an incorrigible liar," "I've never loved you," "You deserve to die alone," "You are a fat slob," and similar direct attacks to your partner's own persona are usually signs your relationship has a 99% chance to be over, sooner or later, or you and your partner will merely survive in an ocean of love unhappiness.

Interestingly, couples who act in contempt against each other are more likely to suffer from infections than more respectful couples.[28]

A forth pattern of poor communication is **defensiveness**. Defensiveness is not acknowledging there is an issue, and it's not accepting any even small form of personal blame. The 'innocent victim' whines that it's not his fault, he did nothing wrong, and instead sends the message that he feels always picked on, despite the many *other* good things he does.

The defensive partner not only does not take any blame; he in fact places the blame back to the attacking partner. "There is no pleasing you" is a common refrain.

The last characteristic of poor communication is **stonewalling**. Stonewalling is a deadly conversational mine. While with criticisms, contempt, and defensiveness there are words exchanges, stonewalling involves the end of the willingness for exchange of views. The stonewalling partner tunes out.

He stops talking. He walks out. In the fight (criticism, contempt, stonewalling) or flight (stonewalling) world, the partner has chosen the latter. Interestingly, **in 85% of heterosexual couples, the stonewaller is the man**. Men are more easily overwhelmed by marital conflict, and evolutionarily they have less patience and resilience. We are after all the weaker sex. This is no excuse, in fact it is an aggravating feature. **We know it, and we still do not fight this despicable behavior.**

The woman instead is constitutionally better able to handle the stress that effective communication can bring. She is more capable to deal with the anxiety that resolving two differing points of view entails. The husband will tend to avoid going deeper in the issue. The wife will demand getting to the bottom of each other's arguments, and attempt positively at an agreeable resolution.

In fact, once she becomes extremely frustrated about a trait of her partner, she'll try negative tactics to try to force him to be more loving. She might withhold her affection and become emotionally distant. She might stop kissing, or hugging with intent. This internal reasoning is that, if she gives their partner enough pain by taking away something she knows the partner longs for, the partner will change.

It's maddening to believe that hurting a partner on purpose on something they really care about, would make them behave better.

People should instead just openly communicate their needs for more affection, time, help, lovemaking, freedom or whatever they need.

This behavior goes back to when we were babies, and the louder we screamed, the more attention we got. Some kids learned that the more they misbehaved, the higher was their chance to get gelato. The success of this tactic became an imprint on our behavior. We think that when we are frustrated, we need to provoke negatively the people around us.

As babies, being as unpleasant as possible may eventually cause someone to come to the rescue. We did not need to explain ourselves much; our caretakers knew what we wanted, being a change of diaper or a videogame as we grew up.

When criticism, contempt, defensiveness, and stonewalling were present in a relationship, a study showed that there was an 84% chance of couple failure.[28]

Poor communication could be mended perhaps by repair attempts. Failure of repair attempts is another sign of a doomed future for a relationship. One partner is still trying to de-escalate arguments and trying to stay calm and positive, but the other is not allowing any truce or attempt at meaningful dialogue.

If despite criticism, contempt, defensiveness and stonewalling, repair attempts are successful, 83% of couples remain together. **With all 5 negative characteristics, i.e. criticism, contempt, defensiveness, stonewalling and inability to repair, 90% of love relationships fail.**[28]

Sue Johnson, in Hold me tight,[12] a great book, describes three basic 'Demon Dialogues,' other examples of poor communications. She also describes possible solutions to overcome demon dialogues when they start.

The **Find the Bad Guy** Dialogue is a dead-end pattern of mutual blame. The purpose of these conversation is self-protection, and the means to self-protection are attack, accusation and blame of the other. The argument both partners are strongly arguing for is, **"It's not me, it's you!"**

The repair attempt should at least involve one of the partners to state, "We are attacking each other, to prove the other one is the bad person. We are just going to get more and more hurt if we continue this pattern of communication. May be we can talk about what happened without it being anyone's fault?"

The **Protest Polka** Dialogue is when one partner becomes critical and aggressive and the other defendant and distant. Studies have shown that couples that get stuck in this pattern of communication have a >80% chance of splitting within 5 years. Relationships fail when there is **decreased emotional responsiveness**.

Often the person who withdraws does not even feel there is much of a problem in the couple; he just remains distant to avoid getting hurt. He feels that whatever he does, won't work. He will just be blamed further. So he does less and less, and retreats into a shell. The other partner of course pokes harder and harder the shell, feeling shut out and alone. Typical is the retreat to the man's cave, or to golf, or to tv.

This toxic pattern of communication can stop with both partners focusing on the issue, and not 'name-blaming' the other. The aggressor should not accuse the defendant, but the fact in itself should be discussed. And the defendant should take the critique not personally, but as a chance to grow and better understand his partner. The dance needs to focus on what moves were wrong, on those details, and not on the fact that the other partner in general is a terrible dancer.

The **Freeze and Flee** Dialogue is a withdraw-withdraw pattern, where the heat is so high so quickly that both partners give up the chance to communicate right away. Emotions cannot be suppressed. This pattern only makes them worse.

It's so sad in a long-term relationship realizing at some point that perhaps you never really got to know all the way, deeply, your partner. She never revealed her true feelings, her most intimate thoughts, the reasons behind her at times unconceivable behavior. What were the ghosts that made your lover behave the way she did? You never discovered them.

She was perhaps not taught to share and be intimate as a child, or was burned in past relationships when she opened up. Now she is a shell who won't let in even her lifelong partner. Sad, so sad. But it happens all the time. And for many of us, it's a cause for long standing unhappiness and depression, or for fleeing the emptiness.

Negativity

Every relationship has its challenges. One key is to accept the simple truth that difficulties will be present, can be worked out, and when they cannot, a mutual understanding and truce can arise, focused on the fact that there are nonetheless so many positives in the relationships.

When a relationship is not going well, one or both partner focus instead on the negatives. For examples, the partner brings back bad memories. With every argument, some ill event and related feeling from the past resurfaces, to make the current argument ever more acid, and bound to fail as well.

When the relationship is in the later stages towards failure, partners often begin to create a mental story of the relationship that **centers around the faults of the other**. One partner becomes stuck in his ways and opinions, unwilling to change, and **just blames the other for everything.** If you are the recipient of such behavior, it might be time to change partner. The blame is almost never just on one side.

Unwillingness to change

First, let's discover if our partner can change at all something we see as **a flaw so big we are willing to end the relationship over it**. If we discover our partner is avoidant, was badly hurt by being unloved when very young, or when an adult, **he may be unable to change**. It's not that he is unwilling.

This person decided a long time ago never to trust someone else in love matters. **She decided never to give anyone the power to hurt her again, to crush her again. They have given humans a chance in the past. They are unwilling anymore.**

That is often unchangeable, and we should accept it and walk away if intimate emotional connection is like air for us, as for most people. Sounds harsh, but it is the only way to at least save ourselves, since our potential partner does not want to be saved, and in fact desires to be left alone.

Some other partners fail to love their own self. If you let yourself go, to lack of self-care, vices, etc, you'll become less lovable. Illicit drugs, smoking, excessive gambling, depression, other mental disorders, sloppiness, poor hygiene, falling into morbid obesity, laziness, losing you job and not looking for another, will make your partner change their mind about you. In these situations, sometimes change is possible; sometimes it's impossible, or just the partner is unwilling. It's important we find out soon.

Partners need to be able to be flexible and adapt to life as it changes. The way things used to be is not a plan for the future. As things change, we need to adapt. We cannot be set in our ways always. There are so many major events in life which change it dramatically.

Some examples are changes in jobs, having kids, kids leaving the house, parents and other loved ones dying, retirement. Many thankfully have the will to adapt, adjust, evolve. If your partner is incapable of changing something too important for you, it might be time to move on.

Classic examples of transformation in life are getting married, having kids, and retirement. Nobody can be more important in your life than your partner. Many make the mistakes to keep too linked to a parent, and lesser the status of the partner compared to a dad, or mom.

Even more common is the mistake, especially for new mothers, to put her kid(s) on top of their affection and priority. **The three years after a baby is born are associated with a 67% drop in marital satisfaction**. There is less sleep, less money, less free time, more tasks, and conflict on how to parent.

The most critical drop in satisfaction is in the first year of life of the child, where lack of sleep and frequent cries and smelly messy diapers reign, no matter how good one parents. Mothers want less sex – like once every few weeks, while fathers pretend the same as before – preferably every other day. Many mothers get postpartum depression, and most of them suffer at least postpartum blues.

Instead strengthening the bond between partners is the best way to face parenthood successfully. Having kids should be a chance to be able to collaborate even more, talk even more, strategize and organize even more. It's a time of reciprocal gratitude for the hard work of incessant tasks and attention to a new defenseless being.

In retirement, suddenly all 24 hours in the day are an opportunity to be together; nothing anymore is in the way, like job or kids. Research shows that in general older couples tend to fight less, have fewer negative emotional responses, and show more affection, even during arguments.[3]

The best tonic for staying healthy in our old age is working on an ever happier love relationship with our partner. The emotional support from a partner we trust completely on, we know we can count on, and who listens well, is priceless. **If we are unable to be happy with our partner in a financially-comfortable and healthy retirement, we are with the wrong partner**.

Repetitive rejection

Unsupportive behavior feels like repetitive rejection, and kills the emotional love bond. Example of these behaviors include minimizing the scope of the problem, discouraging the expression of feelings, offering offhand and unhelpful advice. Such behaviors predict relationship distress.

Your partner avoids you. And when you push for closeness, she rejects you outright. This occurs daily, and most attempts to spend time together, to achieve the emotional and physical intimacy you crave so desperately, are declined by your partner.

While we try to avoid confronting reality, we should instead focus on possible ways your partner is avoiding you. **She reads romance novels all the time. He disappears in the garage. He spends most of the day in his man's cave. She is constantly on the phone with her sister and her friends. He worships the car all day. He plays golf every weekend.**

She is always with the kids. He volunteers for every committee. He spends too much time on the boat. She is too often at her mother's. She watches soap operas in every free moment. He watches sports on

tv or his smart phone all the time. She lives in social media. She claims to be tired or sick all the time.

He finds anything else possible to do but with you. He drinks too much. She does not want to be touched ever. He lives at the tennis club. She jogs all day and then is too tired to do anything else. He goes fishing with his friends forever. She shops all day long. He does not want to move in together. He declines to make love most times you try to.

He is a pot head. She constantly cleans and cares for the house. We keep separate bank accounts. He refuses to get serious, to get married. He reads magazines all evening. She does too many crossword puzzles. He is having an affair.

Too often partners dismiss the other opening up towards them and trying to connect. "**That is ridiculous**" is a statement that not only offends our partner, but lets her retreat from ever opening up again. The rejection to our opening hurts so bad that it ends up catastrophically terminating future intimate connections, and therefore puts an end to any hope of love happiness.

Another important red flag is **being too much into work**, which feels like an excuse not to be together to many partners. In the past this behavior was true especially of men. If men in prior generations had dedicated a bit more time and attention to their wives, instead of being often totally immersed in their work, many domestic partnerships would have been much happier.

The sad part is that often it was the hope of a career, of promotions, of money, that forced those husbands to work so much. When work is instead of a career a calling, with clear high goals, relationships are much better.

Read the biographies of famous men. Trump, one of the richest and at some point the most powerful man alive, has not found love, but a series of short passions, and has made his partners often miserable, most of all probably his current wife.

Elon Musk, often at the top of Forbes list of wealthiest men alive, has also not been able to have a stable, trusted, love happiness relationship. Jeff Bezos of Amazon, and so many others, probably just dedicated themselves too much to career success and too little to relationship success. Perhaps I'm oversimplifying, but I believe there is some truth here.

Even some of the men and women we admire the most stumbled in love. Einstein, Nelson Mandela, Tina Turner, all went through at least one divorce and much heartache in their lives. Many never found a loving mate. Some cheated their way through life, with only an external appearance of marital joy, such as Jack Kennedy.

I bet that on their death beds, many of them will regret the fame and fortune, and miss the walks not taken, the kisses not given, the quality times missed with their loved ones.

There are many exits out of the relationships, while still apparently in a relationship. Often, for most of us, these are escapes from the love disconnection we have at home. The emptiness of the love story is filled with distractions from the pain, the unhappiness. These activities help reduce the underlying despair felt regarding the connection with the partner, but they drain vital energy away from the relationship.

These exits should never be allowed to be formed in the first place if we still have hope of love happiness in our current relationship. They should be closed to allow focus back on the couple. Usually we are conscious enough to know when any of these activities is aimed at purposely avoiding spending time with our partner. There might be good reasons to avoid the partner. It's important to understand these reasons, so we do not have the same behavior in the next relationship.

Emotional connection is vanishing

Do not spend time with someone who does not want to spend time with you.

Gabriel García Márquez

Emotional connection in a relationship, the feeling that your partner understands you, cares for you, listens to you, is and will be always there for you, is the font of all comfort in a romantic relationship. When this emotional bond fades and disappears, that is a clear major sign of trouble.

The common questions we ask inside ourselves when a love relationship is in distress, are all related to the emotional connection not being felt as strongly as initially. "Can I count on you? Can I depend on you? Are you there for me? Will you respond to me when I need you, when I call you? Do I matter to you? Am I valued and accepted by you? Do you need me? Do you rely on me?"

When the person next to us is unavailable, unresponsive, and does not seem to care about our feelings and even about our wellbeing, we are left out in the cold, alone and helpless. Anger, sadness, hurt, and above all, fear, take over. The situation becomes unsustainable.

Eighty percent of divorced couples states that their marriage ended because the gradually grew apart and lost closeness, and because they did not feel loved and appreciated. This is what most commonly kills relationships. Partners seek friendship, support, understanding, respect, attention, caring, and concern.

The **final stages of a relationships usually involve four issues: 1. The couple sees the problems as severe; 2. Talking to solve issues seems to both useless; 3. The couple leads separate emotional lives; 4. Loneliness sets in.**

When partners do get to this stage, then often **extra-relationship affairs occur. The betrayal is a symptom of a dying marriage, not the cause.** It's not about the sex. People are **looking for emotional closeness outside the partnership because they have lost intimacy inside it.**

Women, and men, and others, who cheat, are **often not looking for just hot sex, but more for the emotional connection they have lost** with their partner. Only 20-27% of couples said an extramarital affair was even partly to blame for their failed marriage. Interestingly, now the number of extramarital affairs of young women exceeds that of men.[28]

In fact, non-sexual betrayals can devastate a relationship just as much as a sexual affair. Emotional distance in a relationship may be blamed on personal character of one partner, but **when that partner is found having mental intimacy with someone else, the blow to the relationship is as bad, perhaps worse, as a sexual fling.**

171

The determining factor in whether wives feel satisfied with romance, passion and sex in their relationship is the **quality of the couple's friendship**. Interestingly, this is exactly the same for men. Women and men are actually from the same planet earth after all. **It is the betrayal of the promised mental intimacy that is at the heart of almost every failed relationship**.

Love never dies of natural death. It dies because we do not work at replenishing its source. It dies of ignorance on the principles that work at keeping empathic love alive (Tables 6 and 7). It dies of errors, betrayals, emotional distance, parallel lives.

Red flags

Several 'red flags' can occur even during early parts of a relationship. Most of them are clear examples of rejection, and one partner being avoidant. I'm sharing these illustrations so you can be alert when they occur and get out of the relationships before it's too late. I'll review descriptions compiled from several stories I read or heard to make it easier to review examples.

They met in September. A month or two before, she had seen what she thought was the 'love of her life' relationship end. He was dark, handsome, foreign, sexy, and she was madly in love with him. She lusted over him as she had never lusted over anyone else. But he had ended their relationship, for no apparent reason, at least a reason valid to her.

She recently turned 38 year old. Her mother had married at 20, and had two kids by 24 years of age. She had had several serious boyfriends, but always ended the relationships herself, typical of an avoidant attachment style, until the most recent one. She is very independent, and lives alone, without a boyfriend or a roommate.

Her younger brother had married years before, and the previous year his wife had a son. So she had some family and societal pressure on herself, consciously or unconsciously. Her most recent relationship ended because her boyfriend told her he felt she was like 'ice.'

Indeed many feel they are in a relationship with an emotionally **'Ice King', or 'Ice Queen.'** What is needed in a relationship is not a business partner, a nanny, a financial security blanket, a cleaning lady, a policeman to help keep us safe, a body to have sex with. We need an emotional bond, that's it. Not ice, but rather a soothing warm blanket.

She had heard from her friends that a blond boy from her rural neck of the woods would be a perfect match for her. Now single, shaken from being let go by the prior partner, under family and societal pressures, she agreed to meet him. Friends were routing for them. She accepted his courtship, as she felt accepted, not rejected. Months later, when her parents met him, they were delighted. A good boy, he seemed.

In retrospect, so many factors pushed her to accept his courtship. **She 'rebounded' with him**, she did not want to feel a 'spinster' at 38, she had the strong support of her 'village' of friends and family. Was she in love? Hard to say.

But she felt safe, stable, wanted. Was this really the right direction for her? He had no idea about all this. He was 'head-over-heels' in love with this beautiful, smart girl. He missed all these early signs of possible trouble.

In another couple, when he proposed, she at first did not even 'get it.' He went to his knees, and gave her a small package with inside an elegant diamond ring, and a proposal for marriage, "Will you marry me?" She opened the package, and, beaming of joy at the diamond, said "Thank you!"

Another red flag, but completely overlooked by this other boy. His eyes went sad for a few interminable milliseconds, he told her to please answer the proposal. She said, "Of course, yes." Seemingly she was at first more interested in the ring than him as a person.

In another example, he made sure she understood he wanted to **wait quite a bit before getting married**, after the engagement. There was no rush for him. He was not even sure he wanted to have children. So they eventually set a date about a year and a half after the engagement. Conceivably another red flag. No rush or wish to tie the knot sooner. Lack of commitment should not be taken lightly.

Possibly the biggest red flag in another couple was that, **about three months before the date of the wedding, he told her he was not sure about getting married**. "Why are we getting married? Aren't we happy already like this? There is no need really to get married." She was dumbfounded.

Invitations had been sent out, and friends and family already had arranged to get to the meticulously planned wedding. But this was the least worry for her. She wanted to get married to him. She could not see a better life-move than making official in front of their loved ones their commitment. A long few days passed, and eventually he accepted to keep the weeding plans and date, while she had a few sleepless nights.

People often marry for social reasons. Because 'everyone does it.' Because our siblings did it. Because our parents want us to. Because we want to have a nice party. Because of visa reasons, insurance reasons, economic reasons, rent reasons, shelter reasons. Not for the purpose of making their partner happy.

At the wedding of another couple, the bride's attention was all for the hundreds of guests, in particular for the large number of far-off relatives she did not see often. The groom was almost surprised when at 3am she agreed to come back to their room. Not a romantic wedding.

In another pair, he got **mad when she found out she was pregnant**. While he had been the one to initiate the love making, he held her responsible for getting pregnant again, with their first daughter only a few months old. He blamed her for having another girl too. These two errors on her part were unforgivable. Getting pregnant and with another girl was absolutely inexcusable. He cried from desperation and deep anger. He stopped kissing her from that point on.

She at first did not notice any change. She was so in love. So thankful at her luck of being with him and having two beautiful healthy girls. She was in awe of him. Always. Admired him. Worshipped him. She would ask him occasionally why they were not exchanging real kisses anymore. He would say he did not feel like it. It was not necessary.

In some couples, he retreats over time to less and less physical touch. **He would say, "I do not like physical touch."** She believed him. Much later their kids would remark, "Mom, dad, why aren't you more affectionate?" After many years now, the issue was becoming obvious even to the children; but she still ploughed on.

For decades, in another couple, he had the unconscious feeling of being **rejected**. Of not being enough. Of not being loved. Rejection came in many forms. For example, she preferred to be as far away from him in their huge king bed; in fact, she routinely turned to sleep looking away from him.

Rejection manifested in another couple when he routinely declined to touch lips upon the act of kissing when coming back home. Rejection came for others from declining to go on trips together. To find activities to do together. He thought he was the problem; if she were with someone else, perhaps she'd act more friendly.

She, like other avoidants, found it difficult expressing her desires. She did suppress her needs. Once or twice a year she would burst in anger out of nowhere to him, saying they never talked. As he would engage to this sudden unexpected overture, she would then retreat into herself, unable to really explain what her needs were. Clearly something was wrong for her, but she could not state what.

In other couples, even after a day together doing what he seemed to like, like shopping and having in general quality time together, there is still no wish from him to hug watching a movie, or at least to hold hands. When she approaches the conversation of how to improve the relationship, he routinely finds some flaw in her, **rejecting her even more for trying to get closer.**

While in **couple's therapy**, a partner in another case could reveal that she stopped kissing him for some hidden reason, perhaps after he had 'made her do something she did not like.' Even if she did remember the experience was consensual, in fact initiated by her, and not therefore all his fault.

In these examples, these partners had never seen the red flags which occurred years, often decades earlier. Only now, after years of increasing distance, the sad truth was coming out, finally during therapy. She finally revealed she wound not change. He could either accept her as she was, or else.

Some guys disclose to their psychiatrist that they feel sex with their partner is like sex with an **inflatable doll**; she is so beautiful, so perfectly made. The psychiatrist explains to these guys that they have that image as they are getting nothing emotionally back from their female partner during sex; in fact, she is not kissing him, touching him, she is just there as a doll, getting her quick orgasm without cuddling, without a word of affection.

Moreover, in some couples sex has to be done in complete darkness, in complete silence, always in the same position, with him moving and not much movement from her. There can be nobody in the house, at least not awake.

No other rooms, positions, places are comfortable for him, except the same routine. No novelty is ever allowed, no curiosity, no exploration. When she would propose something even a bit different, he would 'lose' it and yell she was a pervert for wanting more closeness.

In fact, in such situations, he might have treated her the worst, compared to others, because she was the one trying to get close to him. All other people in the world would not pose that treat, and so he would be always nice to them.

He treated her badly because she was the closest, too close. She became his enemy. **The more she tried to get close, the more she got rejected, pushed away, physically and especially psychologically**.

People who are pushed away, rejected in a supposedly romantic relationship, begin being afraid that in an emergency, or even on their death bed, the partner would not be there for them. They begin to realize that they are the person the partner treats the worst.

She could not see herself being on his priority list, as a romantic partner should be. He would belittle her needs. He brushed aside her concerns about their relationship as insignificant. He made her feel inadequate, foolish, to have any requests. She should have realized years prior he did not have her best interest in mind.

This kind of partner, having a secure attachment style, is **prone to forgive**. Prone to keep on trying to make the other happy. Inclined to view her partner's well-being as her responsibility. It's not easy for secure people to call it quit. Hope is their trademark.

They do not realize the avoidant partner is making them lose their secure attachment style; their own partner are making them sad. The whole thing is making them slowly desperate. They do not realize, sometimes never, sometimes late, that both partners would be happier in difference circumstances, apart from each other.

People like them keep on thinking of any excuse, like, "She loves me, but she does not know how to express it," "She is afraid of loving me," "She would love to love me, but can't," or even, crazily, "She loves me, but she does not know it." Love makes us irrational, blind, stupid really. Reality escapes us in these cases. Your love happiness instead should not depend on something you cannot control.

People like them keep on making distancing statements, such as, "I love you, but at this point I am not ready for a relationship," or "I'm blocked from a prior relationship," or "I'm afraid of tying myself too much into you," or "I'm afraid I'll make you suffer," or "I am not worthy of being with you." These all mean they do not want to invest in the relationship, they do not love you.

Unreciprocated love is a disease. We need to cure ourselves of this hopeless situation. No matter how much love we give, or think we give, this will not change our partner. We can try to talk them into love, but it does not work, no matter how long we talk. **You cannot talk people into loving you**. And **there is no one more likely to destroy us than the person who is supposed to be our partner.**

One of the **saddest consequences of feeling rejected** from an avoidant partner when we yearn for love intimacy, is that we become like our partner. We give up on love. We give up on social interactions. We become sad. We become boring. We give up on happiness. We give up on our own dreams. We give up on being our true selves, the biggest sin against ourselves.

It's healthy instead to **accept and face defeat**. 'All hair knots eventually get caught in the hair brush' is an Italian expression to signify that problems eventually either have to get solved, or something else must change. **Pain from a failed relationship, which with maturity we have the courage to move away from, makes us better, wiser persons.**

Some of course compromise. They bury themselves in work. They focus on the positive traits of their avoidant partners. They find refuge in other family members; in friends. **They give up a huge part of themselves, and of their happiness**. They are aware things won't get better; in fact they will probably get worse if there are such differences.

They just hate the idea of being alone, even if there are thousands of better partners out in the world for them. Most **relationships survive just because of the fear of being alone, and the laziness of finding a more suitable mate**. Terrible. Shame on you.

The situation turns at times into a masochistic one. Family and friends notice from the outside your suffering, which is hard to take even for them. They question why the partner is tolerating the bad treatment, and why she is willing to put up with it instead of leaving. They might even think in the end that they deserve it, or perhaps that they like for some reason being rejected, and being unhappy in love. There must be some secret. But there is not.

Some find the **courage to split**, which can be a blessing for both partners. She can find a partner with a secure attachment style. Escape from Alcatraz is priceless. Love happiness is priceless, in my opinion. **Divorce is perhaps the best decision some people ever make**.

It is unwise to stay in an unhappy marriage or relationship for the sake of the children. Even for the kids, a peaceful divorce is preferable to endless marital warfare. Each parent hopefully will be happier out of the negativity of the failed relationship, and will be a better person, a better example for the kids, and a better parent.

Unfortunately, you know so many people who after decades with the wrong person are still together with someone who clearly does not make them happy. Perhaps worse, you have friends who still want to restart a past relationship in which a partner mistreated them, and dumped them, clearly telling they do not love them. Why are we attracted so much to what we cannot have?

Some of the best common sense advice out there is to **work on what you can change; and to accept what you cannot change**, without struggling. Accept a failing, listen to the partner who says (or tells you with his actions) he does not want you anymore. **Accepting a failure we cannot do anything about, is liberating**.

After the split, it's **healthy to stay away from each other**, at least for a while. Both sides need an emotional quarantine from the old partner. Usually only when each finds a new true love, then old partners can begin having some social events together, given the many family ties and common friends left.

Scientific research shows that **a relationship which ended** for important reasons, for character differences, for lack of trust, for attachment style incompatibilities, for differing love languages, **should not be rekindled**. Ever. Those differences which caused the split will resurface again.

Perhaps 1% of prior failed relationships can be fixed; but 99% will stay bad, and perhaps only get worse. Stop getting persistently wounded. Stop wasting your life with someone who is just wrong for you. In fact, stop yearning for some past relationship, maybe with your high school sweetheart, thinking that he was the one that could have made you happy. Regrets, feeling like a victim, pondering on past failed relationships is the wrong way to go through life. Better to build intimacy with someone new, without false hope on prior failures.

The truth is that **a bad relationship can teach us a lot**. The key is to have a few bad relationships, not let them last too long (certainly not decades!), and learn and move on.

In retrospect, looking at the other side of the coin, **we should be very thankful to partners who did not want to start a relationship with us in the past**. I have been lucky that I have not been dumped after starting romantic relationships. But for sure a few women I liked did not allow me to start a relationship with them. While disappointing, they were honest as they were not into me, they did not mislead me, and they saved me time and heartache.

Rejection is so hard on us humans, especially when it comes from the person we thought we were going to spend our life with. There are two very good common reasons why women and men avoid each other. One is anger. The other is fear.

People become **angry** at their partner when their needs are not being met. When they realize their partner is about himself, and his needs, and is not altruistic enough to understand that true love is making her happy the way she likes to be happy. When she realizes that he will never like to go shopping with her. When she gets that he will never voluntarily do the laundry. This creates deep anger.

The other reason for avoiding the partner is **fear**. If your partner does not nurture you and attend to your fundamental needs, a part of you fears that you will die. That you will be alone and wither. So the unconscious reason some people avoid their partners is that they are fleeing death. They see now their partners as enemies who want their death, not to make their life happy.

Love instead is trust, and communication, and openness. **Red flags will appear all along a relationship, usually. The sooner they are dealt with, the better. There should be no dark secrets. No hidden agendas. No undisclosed reprimand for an old misunderstanding**. These bombs only grow more potent over time, and eventually explode.

Here is a pertinent, **wonderful story as told by Mahatma Gandhi**. A wise man from India asked his disciples, "**Why do people shout** at each other when they are upset?" The disciples thought for a while, and one said, "We lose our calm and so we shout!" "But explain to me, why do you shout when the other person is right next to you?" asked the wise man.

"Well, **we shout in order to make sure the other person hears us**," tried another disciple. The wise man asked again, "Isn't it possible to speak to him or her with a soft voice? Why do you shout at a person when you are angry?" The disciples gave some answers but none satisfied the wise man.

Finally, the wise man explained, "**When two people are angry at each other, there is a distance which arises between their hearts**. To cover that distance they must shout, to be able to hear each other. The angrier they are, the louder they will have to shout to hear each other through that great distance."

Then the wise man asked, "What happens when people are in love? They do not shout at each other but talk softly. Why? Their hearts are very close. The distance between them is very small."

The wise man added, **"What happens when their love for each other grows even more? They do not speak, they only whisper. Their hearts come even closer with love. Finally, they need not even whisper... they only look at each other and that is all. That is how close people are when they love each other. Their hearts are like one."**

Nobody is exactly alike to anyone else. Two people will always have some different points of view. How we resolve the points of view shows how much love there is in a relationship. A sign of failure is shouting. Not listening. Never giving up on our right to win the argument. Rejecting our partner.

Another sign of rejection is when you or the other partner is **doing, or being, too much**. Not only too much yelling. But, for example, too much clinging. Not letting the other having her space. Not letting the other practice hobbies which we do not like. **Love, like a human being, dies more often of indigestion than of starvation**.

If you see these signs early, do not start a serious relationship. Do not continue an early meeting. Stories that start on a bad foot usually do not continue well. Recognize people who do not have the traits you are looking for. We should identify the people who we know will hurt us, before allowing them to hurt us. Let's not fall in love with them. Wolves are recognizable often from the start.

A friend of mine, when he first tried to court his now wife of 30 years, got told angrily, **"Fuck off."** The first words they exchanged. Clearly he was up to the challenge, and found rewarding getting married to a tough woman. But I'm unsure that relationship, which started with immediate rejection, has much warmth and reciprocal love.

I actually **cannot stand people who feel like victims**. Who are unhappy, and know why. And do not have the courage to change. Do not blame others. You have the reins of your life, and can certainly find a good mate, because a good mate is out there for sure, as long as you are open, positive, and courageous. You are responsible for your love happiness.

Declining or unsuccessful counseling

I am a huge believer in couple therapy. And research confirms counseling improves romantic relationships open to help. In fact, even happy couples can benefit from professional help. Pardon me the comparison, but this is like anything else. If you need your roof fixed, **best to find a professional who does is for a living, and well**.

You treat a serious illness by going to the doctor. When the car breaks down, it is best to see a professional who knows your type of car and issue well, and does it every day - as much as you may hate to go to the auto shop.

If there is hope of improvement, couple therapy should **continue for about nine months to a year**. There is a lot to uncover and communicate. **If by one year there has been continuous refusal to change, relapse to old negative ways, couple therapy has failed and the relationship will not improve.**

The key moments of change during therapy are those of secure bonding and connection between the partners. Each partner hears the other partner cry for help for renewed emotional connection, and can respond with soothing care, trying to find solutions or coming to understandings.

Sometimes instead counseling clarifies that differences cannot be solved, and **at least one partner unwillingness to change is met by the other partner unwillingness to accept.**

If by one year the benefits of therapy are tangible, the couple can use the new principles themselves for life, going back to therapy occasionally if needed for new or relapsing issues.

Therapy fails when one important issue is identified, and cannot be solved. For example, when one partner wants more intimacy, say by a caress or hug, and the other partner states, "I cannot do it. It's impossible for me. Love me the way I am, I cannot change." If the partner receiving this ultimatum has intimacy as an indispensable need, like for water and food and shelter, the couple has as choices either endless unhappiness or the end of the relationship.

Prevention workshops are those in which couples work on their relationship before any troubles arise. These are three times more effective than workshops for couples already troubled.[28]

I hope many of you who are reading this book are in positive romantic relationships, and are going to improve your love happiness by following the advice in this book. Those who don't believe a word of the research I've written about in this book, probably do not believe love happiness exists. And would probably not benefit from couple therapy, or any other help.

Reasons to go: Too good to go, too bad to stay

About 20% of people in a relationship do not know if to stay or to leave. They see some good things. They see many bad things. They might have had counseling, without making the progress they were hoping for. They have tried counsel from family, friends, but truly nobody can understand as they can, the ambivalence of their situation.

There are **over thirty reasons why you might want to quit your love relationship**, as adapted from Dr Kirshenbaum (Table 10).[34] Even counselors and psychologists are not at all against the couple splitting, if there are good reasons for quitting a relationship, even a long-term one. Let's look at some of these reasons in detail. If one or more of these rings true for your couple, it might be time for you to call it quits.

#1: There was **never a time when things were good**. If looking back at the beginning of the relationship, nothing was good, this is an important negative sign. There is some hope into fixing something that is broken, but it is impossible usually to fix something that never worked. Sadly, for 10% of people in relationships, theirs was never good.

#2: **Physical violence**. In 16% of couples, there is pushing, shoving, slapping, hitting, kicking, and beating up. Severe violence such as hitting with a fist or an object occurs in 6% of couples. You should have ZERO tolerance for this, and run out of that relationship and house ASAP.

#3: **Look at what you are doing**, not at what you are saying. Have you **already made a concrete commitment to pursue a course of action**

or lifestyle that definitively excludes your partner? If you are acting like you are leaving the relationship, it means you know unconsciously that the best for you is to leave. Accepting a job on the other side of the country, having an affair, can be signs of you having made the decision already.

#4: **If somebody gave you permission, you would leave.** This might relate to religious people. They might feel that God wants them to stay, as marriage should not be destroyed, kids should not be let go through divorce, because our mother and/or father does not want us to. You feel responsible to some rule by someone else; you do not want to let down someone. But what if you had all the permissions you needed? Would you then leave?

#5: **There is not even one pleasure activity or interest you share** (besides children). There is nothing you do together that you both like and look forward to do, because it makes you feel close. Sex here counts only if it makes you feel emotionally close. Examples are many, and include having friends over for dinner, dancing, vacationing together, etc. Real love needs real loving experiences. It needs regular positive pleasurable connections. If there is nothing you look forward to do together, you should probably leave.

#6: **Your partner is not nice; he is not smart, he is neurotic, and he does not smell good**. It's harder to love someone who is mean, dumb, crazy, stinky. Interestingly, smell is the most emotional of senses. The first compliment I got when I met my wife, the first time we talked, was that I smelled good. I did not understand it then, as I was wearing no cologne or deodorant. Now I know how important that spontaneous comment was.

#7: **Your partner wants all the power.** Does your partner bombard you with difficulties when you try to get even the littlest thing you want? When you eventually might get what you want, does it feel like the ordeal made it an unsavory experience? Power people poison spontaneity. They poison your well-being. They poison the people around you too – e.g. the kids. Power people poison passion.

#8: **You feel humiliated and/or invisible in your relationship**.

#9: **Your partner does not let you talk about things that are important to you**. Your partner keeps things off the table, blocks you from bringing up certain topics, or questions that you care about. Examples could be avoiding the subject of sex, or never saying, "I love you," or just refusing to clean up. Sexual problems are not separate from relationship problems. If these are important issues to you, there must be an open conversation about them.

Instead, in these cases your partner yells at you for even bringing up the conversation, "What's wrong with you?" it's her angry reply at your requests. Or she just changes the subject at your every attempt. You get left with a sense that you are not worth it, you just get shut up as if you were an idiot for even thinking this is an item for discussion. You would love to visit your parents, but even the conversation is taboo.

People who are in good long-term empathic love relationships often can say sincerely, "We could always talk about anything." This buys you a lot of happiness.

#10: **Your partner lies**. Lying is to communication what murder is to life. If you have gotten to the point that you cannot trust what your partner says, and often feel that it's more likely he is lying than he is telling the truth, this is another motive for leaving. I'm not talking about one lie. I am talking about repeated lies about issues that are important to you. In fact, the badness of the lie is directly related to how bad an impact what he has said, has had on you. It's a pattern of lying.

#11: **One of the partner does not like the other**. In spite of admirable qualities, efforts to spend quality time together, perhaps counseling, you just do not like your partner. Or your partner really does not like you. **No like, no love**. This is a bit like when people talk about the chemistry of love. No chemistry, no future.

#12: **You do not feel like you want to altruistically give to your partner anymore**. Love is first and foremost giving our partner what she desires. If you are not willing to give unconditionally to your partner, that is a major red flag. **When there is nothing left to give, there is nothing left at all**. This could mean even simple things as not feeling anymore like smiling when your partner comes home. Or loving her with her favorite love language. Of offering to help in something she needs to do.

#13: **You never touch each other**. Wanting to touch and wanting to be touched are the bedrock of your physical relationship on which your emotional relationship builds. If your partner instead makes your flesh crawl, it's time to crawl out of the relationship.

#14: **There is no person-specific sexual attraction**. Being attracted to your partner specifically, means there is something special about your relationship.

#15: **Your partner neither sees nor admits the very issues you have been trying him to acknowledge as these make your relationship bad**. If you partner does not even see and acknowledge the important things you are trying to discuss, there is a good chance he'll never see them or admit them or accept to discuss them.

In many such cases, you start getting the sense that even mentioning the problem makes things worse, not better. **If your partner can't even see what it is about him that makes you want to get out, it's time to get out**.

#16: **Your partner admits to what you think is bad in the relationship, but he clearly is not willing to do anything about it**. Willing is the key word here. A good advice may be to score time: ask your partner by what date he is willing to come your way – say lose weight, shower more often, do the dishes, whatever.

If you have tried for many months to come to a compromise about an essential issue, and you feel your partner just keeps coming up with any excuse not to come your way, it's perhaps time for you to go the other way.

Your partner by his behavior is giving you permission to end the relationship. The partner is aware of the issue. The partner made it clear over much time he won't come to a compromise. He knows how strongly you feel about it. When you leave, he'll be keener to understand why.

#17: **You just cannot let go of the vital problem you see in the relationship**. One way to solve a discord, is for you to let go, once you see your partner won't let go herself. Sometimes you can actually come to terms with it, understand the positives vastly outweigh this negative, and let the issue fly away. After all, nobody is perfect.

In a healthy relationship, people can let go of the problems that they cannot solve and that perhaps are not as basic as you thought they were at the beginning. Obviously this should not happen with issues like violence, neglect, domineering, and lack of communication in general. If the problem is essential to you and unresolvable, the exit door may be the only solution left.

#18: **You partner may be willing to change, but he is unable to change**. For whatever reason, may be genetic, may be character, may be peer-pressure, may be anxiety, your partner is unable to quit smoking – as an example, and that's a hard stop for you.

You have made sure your partner knows how much the issue matters to you. You went to therapy, you tried science, medicines, whatever. It's the ability to change that turns frogs into princes. If you are stuck seeing a frog when he smokes (for example), you better get out of that pond.

#19: **Your partner crossed your personal bottom line**. Please figure out your personal bottom lines for you: respect; no violence; trust; no lies; whatever; we are all so different. If you partner crossed your bottom line, you have to act on it. If you do not act on it, you perform an act of self-mutilation.

If he does something that ruins irreparably the relationship for you, you have to hold him responsible. **Do not become an accomplice by finding excuses for him**. Your complicity makes you feel, consciously or subconsciously, like you have betrayed yourself. It's psychologically devastating.

Only *you* know what is the bottom line for you. For examples, no cuddling, preferring others to your company, no help with everyday tasks, or others. **These are issues you are just not willing to live with for the rest of your life**. Defying a bottom line is a relationship deal breaker. Best is to tell your partner clearly ahead of time what you bottom lines are. Some bottom lines you'll discover along the way; and as you do, communicate them to your partner.

#20: **Your partner is different from you in a certain aspect, and you can't live with that**, even if his preference would be acceptable to others. The most common of these differences, but not all, are related to lifestyle:

- Active/lazy
- Hot/Cold
- Urban/rural
- Optimist/pessimist
- Extrovert/ introvert
- Saver/spender
- Intellectual/social media
- Rich/poor
- Practical/dreamy
- Left/right political views
- Different attachment styles
- Different love languages
- Having kids/not having kids

Lovers do best when they have common lifestyles. When they go biking together. When they take walks in the wild together. Not when the other instead prefers shopping, or watching tv series. In this situation, **you feel your partner is too dissimilar from you**; you perceive him as an alien.

Instead, **in successful couples, each partner** can see themselves somehow into their partner. You **feel a deep down similarity with your partner that bonds you to her**. Somehow, when you look down into your partner's eyes, you see part of yourself, the part you like about yourself. A profound similarity can overcome lots of small differences.

If you feel your partner is a Martian from another planet, that should be a red flag.

#21. **You consider the alternative to staying in your current relationship, and, looking at the real options, they are doable and a major improvement**. No relationship is perfect. So your next relationship won't be perfect either. Ask your friends if they think what you aim for in the next 'love life' is a dream, or a possible reality.

This includes facing the issue of loneliness at least for a while. Facing financial hurdles. Moving. Finding a new place. New friends. Different relationship with your kids. Different in-laws eventually. Facing your own village and how they will readjust their relationship with you. If leaving makes sense when you look at the real facts, then it's time to leave.

#22: **Your partner makes you feel as a nut, or a jerk, or a loser, or an idiot**. Your partner does not praise you; she disrespects you. This happens as commonly in women as in men as in LGBTQIA+. Your partner should be your strongest fan, should show you the most respect and admiration.

When you feel you do not want to spend time with your partner out of fear of disrespect, it's time to go. Listen if your kids or friends or relatives are telling you this. You should stop drinking poisonous water, or at least you try to avoid it at as much as possible.

#23: **Your partner does not show clear concrete support for the things you are trying to do, the things that are important to you**. Your partner should be there when it counts. Your partner won't always be able to help, but he should help on the things that matter to you, and respect your wishes and choices.

#24: **You feel you will not lose something important if your relationship ends**. One of the strong feelings people have after their divorce from a relationship that had no hope, is that the interaction after the divorce is similar to the one before. Civil discourse, but no true sharing of feelings, or of human warmth and personal support.

You feel that nothing your partner does for you, truly makes you feel special, loved, appreciated, cared for. The person you dedicate your life to, should be a resource for you. Do not let others influence you on this; it is only *what you perceive* your partner is to you, that matters.

#25: **There is a past hurt from your partner that you will never able to get over**. A past affair, a betrayal, a major lie: the hurt and pain has stayed with you, and months and years have not lessened it. About 20-25% of women and men admit in anonymous surveys to have had physical affairs while in a serious relationship; and 40% admit they have had 'adulteries of the heart,' at least 'dreaming' and imaging having an affair.

Time heals healable wounds, but not all wounds are able to heal. It depends how you feel about it. If after say 5 years, you still hurt, and you spend 50% of your time in pain, and 50% still trying to forgive but being unable to, then that is a red flag. On the other hand, not all affairs have to end a relationship.

There are so many details, and so many different ways we approach these relationship wounds and we feel about them. This also relates to forgiveness. Are the partners able to forgive themselves on smaller things? Is one partner just unable to let go ever, even for example regarding the fact you forgot the light on in the garage last night?

#26: **Your partner is unable to forgive**. Has your partner been able to forgive someone in the past after being hurt? Has your partner been able to forgive you for something they disagreed with? There will always be moments of difficulty in a relationship. You as a partner will at times fail and therefore hurt your partner.

Each partner must be able to not only as the perpetrator, express being sorry and feel genuine apology, but also when the receiver of the hurt, be able to forgive. Without forgiveness, you cannot find a way to get close emotionally again. There is nobody more unhappy than the person who cannot forgive.

#27. **You are unable as a couple to negotiate solutions when disagreements and problems arise**. Members of a successful couple feel safety inside the relationship. Each feels the partner understands, and can discuss positively solutions. A good partner is someone who can see our most important needs and 'come' towards us, not against us.

But many couples reach a point where a cold war ensues in which there is emptiness, inability to communicate, to collaborate, to compromise. If you have a reasonable personal need, your partner should be able to work out a way for you to fulfill that need without much of a struggle.

If you lose hope to have your loved one really be a partner in making you happy, then your relationship is over. It should not be an ordeal just to discuss the littlest things. You need to be able to sit down together and talk things out, finding solutions and compromises that are win-win for both, as much as feasible.

If your partner is always tired, and never agrees to cuddling, and that is vital for you as much as food and air, then the relationship might just not work out. Not only: your partner must be able to agree to a consensual agreement, and then put facts to words, maintain the promises she made.

What seems like politeness in a couple may be despair: the partner has been unable for years to negotiate any solutions to the couple's major problems, and has given up, showing outside politeness that really means she has surrendered any hope of love happiness.

It's actually better to 'fight' if that leads to a fruitful outcome agreeable to both. It's not the fighting itself but the unmet needs of the fruitless arguing that means it's time to leave. Frustration, fear and deprivation are nature's way of telling you the relationship is not a good one for you, and you should get out of it.

In particular, your 'big' need must be met. There are some things you cannot live without. Some things without which your life loses meaning. Those should be facilitated by your partner. You cannot have a fulfilled life without your basic needs.

Your partner should help you along in your quest for your dreams. These are all different for each of us. They could be having love happiness itself, kids, extended family, volunteer work, professional aspirations, whatever. Your partner should be aware of the needs you cannot live without, and help you fill them.

#28: **When you get close, your partner hurts you**. Mutually agreeable escalating nakedness means sharing ever more with time our most inner thoughts and 'secrets.' We should feel safe that our partner is the one person able to understand us, forgive us, help us. If instead, when we bear our soul to our partner, he uses our moment of emotional sharing to hurt us, it's time to go.

If you feel your partner seeks closeness to be able to then attack you with criticism and anger, you are with the wrong partner. Your partner may be filled from the past with hate and destructiveness: don't let him pour that on you. You don't deserve that, and he'll never change unfortunately.

#29: **You cannot get to intimacy with your partner**. Emotional, even more than physical, intimacy is the biggest price in a positive love relationship. Is there a battle in your relationship over what intimacy is? Does he just want sex, while you seek long walks talking about everyday struggles and feeling your partner is listening?

Does your partner refuse to say "I love you," and that drives you insane? Your partner may actually think, and even say openly, that your vision of intimacy is a mistake, is dangerous. If using a lubricating gel is considered depraved by your partner while you were only trying to help her vaginal dryness in menopause, that might be an unbridgeable divide.

Your partner may have a completely different opinion of what intimacy his; please find out sooner rather than later if you agree or disagree on this. **If getting close drives you apart, you can never get close.** To hear from your loved one that what you think genuinely as a possible solution is wrong and despicable, and you should be ashamed for even thinking it, is truly a deal breaker.

#30: **There is no more fun, or even hope for fun, in the relationship.** Being together is supposed to make you feel good. If instead you feel gloom and despair by being with your partner, that is a clear red flag. Laughing, joking and fooling around should remain in some form and in some moments of your love relationship forever. Forever.

Losing the hope that fun will ever come back in your relationship means it's time to go. **Fun is different for each of us.** But we need it. **Whatever fun is for you, fun is the orgasm of intimacy.**

#31: **You have no more shared goals and dreams with your partner.** Having a house? Having kids? Raising them a certain way? Sharing time with friends? Helping family in need? Volunteering for a common cause? Whatever they are, shared goals hold us together.

#32: **Even if all your relationship problems were solved today, you still feel ambivalent if to stay or to leave.** If you don't know if you want to stay even if nothing were wrong, then you do not want to stay.

Getting to despair

There are about 5 phases of the **power struggle** between lovers.[6] After passionate love, empathic love opens our eyes and we discover the inescapable inevitable flaws of our partners.

The **first stage is shock.** We had believed in a perfect individual, and now we discover the many imperfections. It's like meeting a whole new different person. Distinct from the ideal one we had first fell madly in love with.

The **second phase is denial**. We do our best to see our partner negative traits in a positive light. We try to pretend the flaws are not so important. Or perhaps the flaws can be smoothed out. Or at least the many more virtues can temper the minor flaws.

The **third phase is betrayal**. We feel our partner has changed, we cannot remember these flaws which must have been acquired at our detriment. Or even worse, we feel our partner deceived us by having hidden these major flaws at the start of the relationship, as we were gullible during blind infatuation.

The **fourth phase is bargaining**. "If you stop golfing every weekend, I'll make love to you tonight." "If you do the dishes, I won't complain all the time about you eating too much." We try to correct the flaw by giving some reward for the desired behavior. With good communication and understanding, this might work at times, and at least communicate the needs clearly, and their importance.

The **last phase is despair**. There has been not enough improvement, and we lose completely any hope for the idyllic relationship we had dreamed of all our life, especially in the passionate phase. There are no longer any hopes of finding love happiness within the relationship. We now fear loneliness, abandonment, solitude, death; at the least intimacy death.

Sadly, some studies show that **as few as 5% of all couples find a way to resolve their power struggle** and go on to create and enjoy a deeply satisfying love relationship. Many people are living in an **invisible divorce**. The relationship is non-existent. The emotional needs are met outside the relationship. For example via a friend, a relative, religion, a fling outside the union that has become a non-union, a separation.

Separation and Divorce

I grew up being taught that divorce was like a curse word. Divorce was described as awful, divorcees to be shamed and distanced, as a terrible example to a young child. My view of divorce has changed 180 degrees in my life. If separation and divorce are the way to end a relationship devoid of empathic, emotional connection and mutual intimate support, with the hope to still pursue love happiness with someone else, then separation and divorce are courageous acts to be admired.

There are some things that are just not fixable. We need to learn to fight for what can be improved, and to give up and admit defeat when change and improvement are no longer possibilities. Examples are a partner unwilling to be emotionally close; a partner who has cheated, and even denied it; a partner who says something so hurtful, that there are no apologies that will ever erase it.

Model phrases that lead to couple dissolution are, "I never loved you," "I am not attracted to you anymore," "You are a self-centered asshole," "You are a bitch," and so on; you get the sense.

Without following the suggestions given in this book (Tables 6,7,12,13), most of us will fall in love with the wrong person. Our planet is full of people who remain alone even if paired, who suffer, who cry from depression and desolation. Some of them even think they are in a romantic relationship, unaware that they have never really tasted love happiness.

Humans now live longer; stay healthier longer; baby boomers and all others value personal happiness; women finally have the financial means to live of their own. All these factors make it more possible for unhappy partners to get out of what's not working. **As partners in a couple we should try to 'make it work' as much as humanly possible; but, as we have seen** (table 10),[34] **sometimes couple's issues are not mendable in a mutually agreeable and satisfactory way.**

Not every adult is made to enjoy love happiness. Avoidants may need to change partners as things get too close. While all of us humans need the emotional and physical closeness of love happiness, some grow into adults who have given up on this pursuit.

Moreover, naturalists report in studies that **only 7% of mammals are monogamous.** An anthropologist studied 853 different *human* cultures, most clearly not part of Western 'civilization,' and found that **only in 16% of them monogamy was preferred, or expected.**[35] She actually concluded that humans are polygamous, and only culture makes us monogamous. Interestingly, 90% of birds are monogamous.[3] I'm glad my sister and brother-in-law call themselves 'seagulls in love.' It makes sense, they have been together 38 years.

Some insists that humans are naturally monogamous.[3] Nature has indeed designed us so that physical closeness easily leads into bonding and caring. Sex is one of the initial hooks into a relationship. Some aspects of our physiology do not correlate with monogamy.

For example, why do males continue to ejaculate over 20 million spermatozoa with each orgasm from puberty until over 80 years old, decades after their partner's menopause?

Studies show that **almost half of all US men and women cheat on their mate, and about half get divorced**. The majority of the times the reason is that the bond with our partner is not good, the match was not worthy to begin with, or has deteriorated.

In these situations we feel lonely even if technically still in the relationship, and we seek intimacy somewhere else. The intimacy sought may look to be physical, but truly we are seeking the emotional closeness we are not getting with our current partner.

Kids together should not be the reason to stay together. Divorce is separation from a partner, not from your kids. Parenting continues. And often parenting is better than before, as we are more serene, and the kids experience less tension, less conflict, less yelling. Kids also enjoy more one-on-one moments with each of their parents, which is the best way we can relate to each other.

I grew up thinking that divorce was evil: I did not even meet my first degree cousins, the only sons of my father's only brother, until I was 15, as they were both divorced (they were older than us) and therefore 'terrible examples.'

One of them is named Vincenzo Berghella, like me. When I started high school, the teacher asked me to say hello to Marcello Berghella, the younger cousin, and I did not know what to say as I did not know him. Such was the shame of divorce in families in 1970's Italy.

Perhaps you are unhappy, but still fear divorce. For some, divorce is the best decision in their life. Certainly the most courageous. To leave a nest which is tidy, predictable, professional in its routine, and a man who is beautiful, raised wonderful children, and keeps a spotless house, it's hard. It is such a brave choice to want to make someone else happy, when you realize your partner does not want to be.

There are many reasons why couples end up separating. Common reasons for divorce are listed in Table 11. Certainly the **lack of a strong emotional bond** is a reason that encompasses many others. One or both partners feel they cannot count on the other for their emotional needs. The emotional responsiveness of our partner is low or non-existent, so that we feel alone and unsupported even if, technically, in a relationship. This is a classic sign of an unsecure attachment, which is painful and the cause for much negativity.

Should you quit your current relationships? Should you get a divorce? This quiz https://www.marriage.com/quizzes/should-you-get-a-divorce-take-this-quiz-and-find-out might help. Reviewing Tables 10 and 11 is also useful.

Separation and divorce should be lived differently in our Western culture. In the Sahara's Tuaregs, for example, when a couple wants to divorce, a big village party is thrown. This makes the necessary pain more sharable, with more support. And three months later, as now the woman knows she is not pregnant, another party is thrown, with the additional purpose to entice new possible partners.

Love depends on you

Love is an action verb.
Suzanne and James Pawelski

Love doesn't just sit there, like a stone, it has to be made, like bread;
remade all the time, like new.
Ursula K. Le Guin

Love is an emotion. But more importantly love is also good sense.
Adapted from Ken Kesey

Man can't choose his birth, but he can choose his mate.
Mandragola

Love is proved by deeds; the more they cost us, the greater the proof of
our love.
Mother Teresa of Calcutta

Men don't seduce; women choose.

Don't wait anymore for love to come to you. Choose to love. Learn to love. You can no longer wait for things to get better by themselves. Do not compromise your love happiness waiting for things to magically change. Be realistic. Do not dream of solutions you have already tried in the past, and failed numerous times. Love requires action. Love requires effort. Love requires altruism.

Liberate your energy to actively work to improve your relationship, or seek a different one if you have found through this book that your current one is unfixable, and you just can't live with it. Identify your problems, and actively solve them. You only can do this for yourself.

One should pick her mate based on **certain important characteristics**, which are not the ones we usually use to pick our mates (Tables 3,5,6,7,12,13). Historically, and bombarded now by TV and

197

social media stereotypes, we pick our partners based on physical and status characteristics. We instinctively pick mates who will enhance the survival of the species, and in particular the health of our own progeny.

Studies do show that some **women instinctively favor males with 'alpha' qualities, those that show that he can dominate other males**. So being tall, muscular, fit, with broad shoulder, becomes attractive. But also having wealth, being in a professional position of power, is attractive to women, who see the older chairman of the board as one being able to support her future kids well.

Men are in general more concerned with mating with a woman who will have a healthy pregnancy and therefore a healthy baby. So males often look for wide hips, big breasts, curvy complexion, as these qualities may indicate youth and good health, signs that a woman can bare healthy children. I'm an obstetricians, and I can assert this is not based on scientific evidence.

Some also chose their mates according to an 'exchange theory.' We size our partner's up for physical appeal, financial status, social rank, perhaps some personality traits. And then we tally up how equivalent we are, so to make the trade fair.

Some look instead to enhance their self-esteem. "How would I look next to this person?" She is tall, thin, beautiful, if I can make her my partner I'll look good to my parents, siblings, friends, co-workers, strangers. There is some element of selecting a mate based on trying to enhance our self-image.

Other qualities instead, or at least in addition, should be more important, for long-term love; but they are often overlooked (Tables 6,7).

Having now read this entire book, you might realize you have made some mistakes in the past - and perhaps in your present too - in love relationships. I certainly have. I have learned a lot though. I feel I have the recipe now. I have the cook book to grow a wonderful intimate love happiness bond with someone. In fact, I have already. And writing and rereading often in the past, present and future this book has helped me and will help me stay on course.

Knowledge is power. I hope the principles in this book will help you achieve love happiness. I hope you have realized that if there are issues in your current (or past) relationship, it's probably not because you are crazy, but because your relationship has a built-in clash – e.g. in attachment style, love language, etc, that is not going to go away.

I hope you have now realized **how wonderful you are**. You are an angel with one wing. To get the second wing and fly to love happiness with someone else, the first step is believing in yourself, and your self-worth. **Your first soulmate in life should be yourself.** Be confident, positive, know your strengths and what you need. Tell yourself, "I love myself. I am capable of loving. I want to receive love. I am Love." Only knowing we are love, we can attract love.

Hopefully you have realized your attachment style (Table 2), your preferred love languages (Table 3), your essential love factors (Table 6), and what it takes to have a positive successful romantic long-term relationship (Table 7). In brief, hopefully now you know who you are and what you need.

It's not even what you want. It's what you *need*. Now you can better identify the person with the characteristics that can bring you a chance at love happiness. Once these align to your liking, let yourself fall in love. A key element of love happiness is being able to give in into the **revolution** that falling in love represents.

Falling in love involves losing oneself into the other, and so exposing oneself to rejection, failure, and great pain. I have met many persons, mostly over 35 year old but sometimes even younger, who have lost the courage to fall in love. Some admit they have lost hope, too.

Revolution, really. Think about it. A new partner usually brings a new way of life, a new inherited family, often a new dwelling, different car, friends, economic situation, joys and sorrows. Nothing is as revolutionary in your life as a love partner. **Don't be afraid of being liberated from the prison you are in, and join the revolution you have been dreaming about since you were a baby.**

Be sincere with yourself. You'll miss what you'll leave behind. You'll feel like you jumped in the unknown at first. But if you follow your heart, and importantly the principles highlighted in this book, you'll come out ahead eventually, and live the existence you want for yourself. **True love wins in the end, every time – if you let it and if you work at it.**

Indeed love is the contrary of a guarantee. The loved one may fall out of love. She may betray you. He may hit you. They may die unexpectantly. All after we have dedicated our whole life to them. Love altruism is a lot of work, and it comes naturally only to some of us.

Look around. Look at your family. Look at your friends. How many have truly positive love relationships, as far as you can judge from the outside? Probably very few, if any. Blissful **romantic love is rare. It is difficult**. But it is possible. It just requires you to follow the steps in this book!

Love relationships, the true happy long-lasting ones, take courage, determination, resilience. Love has so many benefits (Table 2). Love is the best anti-depressant.

Do not live in a dream world. **Experience has thought each of us that perfection does not exist**. It is best to embrace this reality, and know *any* **partner would have flaws**. Start by knowing what you want and who you are, and what you most desire in your partner. Do not focus on what's missing in your mate and do not overlook her fine qualities; do not take those abilities for grated; others do not have them. Search for reasons to praise, not to criticize.

Here is a test to understand if you are with the right person. **The difference between loving and liking is that if you like someone, you can be without him; if you love him, you cannot live without him.** I feel this way about Federica. I cannot live without her. I love the way she makes me feel. She allows me to love her. I love the way she loves me. She makes me a better person; she gets the best part of me out.

Expressing your needs and expectations to your partner in a direct, non-accusatory manner is a powerful tool to achieve the love you want, and deserve. In order to be happy in your relationship, you need to find a way to **communicate your attachment needs** clearly without resorting to attacks or defensiveness. And you need to listen carefully to the emotional needs and the description of the attachment style of your partner.

Using secure attachment style strengths helps, too. Secure individuals are great conflict busters. They are mentally flexible. They are effective communicators. They can discuss their emotions openly, and coherently. They do not play games. They are comfortable with closeness, intimacy, and aren't afraid to becoming 'enmeshed' with another human, their partner.

They are quick to forgive, and assume their partner's intentions are good. They feel responsible and therefore work on their partner's well-being. **They know, deep inside, their partner's happiness is their happiness**.

It's easy then to understand if your relationship has a chance. **If your partner shows a sincere wish to understand your needs and to put your well-being first in his life, then your future together looks bright and hopeful**. You can give this relationship the green light to evolve and proceed forward.

If instead he brushes aside your needs as insignificant, or makes you feel inadequate, foolish, or self-indulgent, you can quickly conclude that this person does not have your best interests in mind, and you are probably incompatible, no matter how much you'll try.

Do not interpret the insecure person excuses, or attacks, for something you are perfectly fit to fix. You will most probably fail, as they do not want to get fixed, they are fine as they are as far as they themselves are concerned. Just because you think you deserve to be loved, it does not mean the other person can see that, understand that, embrace that, be able to love you the way you want. It might be like asking a math genius to like poetry the most, or vice versa.

Never believe that your needs are illegitimate. Whether they are legitimate or not for someone else is not the point at all. Your needs are essential for your happiness, and that is what's important. You need to find someone who can hold your bare soul in his hand, keep it safe, and make it happily prosper. Do not let your soul be in solitary confinement; our souls are social creatures who need nurturing, just like when we were babies.

Merit. Don't forget merit. **Your merit**. If you got to this last part of the book, it means **you still believe in love**. It means **you have something to give**. If someone could not give you want you need, it means that either they could not because of how they are, or they were not in love with you. Those people do not deserve you. You deserve the best.

There is more good news. **There are many, probably thousands if not millions, of wonderful individuals in the world who can make superb partners for you**. There are many charming intelligent caring people who can make you happy. You just have to choose well, and stay away from the many (thousands, probably millions) of people who are not right for you.

Do not waist time with someone who is unkind to you, when there are many potential partners out there who would treat you like royalty; like you want to be treated. Make your choice before the point of no return, being financial, religious, as you get linked to a house, kids or whatever else is critical for you.

In a study, **73% of university students stated they were willing to sacrifice the majority of their goals in life for a positive romantic relationship**. I stated so when I was a teenager, in my diary. Do not leave the success or failure of your love relationships to chance. **Empathic long-term love relationships are *the* most rewarding of human experiences**, above and beyond other gifts that life has to offer.

Do not be guided by misconceptions and myths. Be guided by the scientific principles I did try to summarize in this book. Like everything else in life, go grab your love happiness. *You* make it happen. It's not luck; it's effort and planning and finding cogently the right mate to lose yourself passionately with.

Love happiness is a path, a journey of continuous striving for these issues:

- Find your true identity, what you attachment style is, what your love languages are.
- Understand your emotional need are legitimate.
- Find someone similar to you, in general.
  - Similar in believing in love in the first place.
  - Similar in love languages.
  - Similar in your secure attachment style.
- Let yourself depend on your partner's love. This will make you feel self-confident, and give you peace of mind for the challenges of life.

- Express your love needs and expectations honestly and directly to your partner, with constant open positive communication.
- Be aware that we are all different, and not everyone has the same capacity for love intimacy. If your needs go unmet, it's not necessarily your fault, but possibly something to do with your partner. It's not their fault to be different, and perhaps not made to make you love happy
- Understand what your partner's love needs are, and show and prove your concern for her well-being. Her well-being equates to your love happiness! (and vice versa ☺)

Love happiness is **hard work**. Many people meet someone and expect that by magic all their troubles will disappear, and that their love dream will become reality. Instead it's when empathic love starts that the hard work starts. We are the only ones who can make our love happiness dream become reality, via the tools highlighted in this book.

Love happiness **requires action**. Just like happiness requires action.[1] It takes constant, daily, continuous effort to know who we are; to learn every day better what our partner likes. To practice the qualities that are known to be associated with better relationships (Tables 6, 7). To cultivate positive emotions, such as joy, gratitude, hope, serenity, and love.

Love happiness **will not fall freely from the sky**. You and your partner both have to work really hard at it. Dancing smoothly, bidding for each other's attention and receiving it. Be open to present moments, to savoring the special events, avoiding what creates friction. **Dancers are carefully attuned to each other. They discover and then cultivate each other's strengths. They alternate smoothly and beautifully initiation and response.**

Building a long-term successful love relationship is like **building a muscle**. We need to go regularly to the love gym. We need to put our time in cultivating our relationship. We must aim for continuous improvement, knowing that perfection is impossible. We should aim for the best possible love relations for us and our partner. Connecting and supporting the good we see in our partner and in ourselves.

It is **unfortunate that for many of us, the focus of life is more what happens outside the house, than inside it**. Our culture focuses on achieving power, success, wealth, status, so we can post it on social media and boost our ego. The main focuses of human life should be that parents love their children unconditionally and warmly, and that adults practice with their partner the skills I've reviewed in this book. True happiness is in our closest social relationship.

In fact, **we can only have success outside the home if we are first successful in our original family where we were raised, and then in securing the same love bond with our one love partner**.

You can make love last because now you know how to repair it, and renew it (tables 6,7). The more you believe that you can positively influence your relationship, first by modifying what to do, the harder you will now try to keep it not only alive, but thriving. After all, it will only benefit you! The more effective your efforts, the happier your life will become.

I do not think luck is backed by any evidence. What happens in your life, to a great degree, depends on your choices. Love happiness can only be achieved with hard work in finding out first who you are (Tables 3,5).

Long-term happiness is achieved with your heart, but **even more with your mind** (Tables 6,7). What one small thing can you do today and every day from now on and forever to make your lover feel that you want her happiness, that you will always be there for her?

Many stay childishly at passionate love, the first short-lived stage, thinking that it can last for a long time. It can't. From the initial romantic infatuation, love should evolve to an **open discourse on how to navigate differences and enjoy similarities in likings and passions**. Love should become a reciprocal need, when we feel like we belong to each other, and we can live well with the imperfect partner, who we love despite the flaws. Empathic relationships culminate in a conscious altruistic love of the other, knowing only a happy lover can make us a happy lover.

Love must be continuously fed. Change is the norm. Humor, fantasy, flirting with each other even after 40 years together: these are tips for long-term success. Love is like a plant. Or like our health. It needs continuous attention. Without proper watering, light, soil, a plant dies. Without proper nutrition, exercise, our health deteriorates. Love needs certain essential elements (tables 6,7).

You cannot retain your baby attitude, when your mother and father loved you unconditionally no matter what you did. As an adult, love happiness requires your effort too. And when both you and your partner work at the principles of love happiness, you achieve it! While there can be love when one altruistic partner loves the other who instead behaves like a selfish baby, true long-term empathic love happiness is reached only when both partners practice empathic love.

Another important point to achieve love happiness is to **never give up**. A major key is not to accept the status quo. It's to grow together. To evolve with time. Pre-kids. During childcare times. After empty nesting, when the happiness can further increase by being able to have more time and money to do exactly what you like to do.

Some of us, but not all of us, have an **irresistible need to love**. For those who believe in love, **love is a risk worth taking. Nobody is unlucky in love**. Unlucky in love is the one who does not dare to get hurt, to try, to discover what she likes, to join an attitude of giving, expecting nothing back. Lucky in love is the **altruistic audacious cuddler who follows exactly her dreams**.

In the end, will you prefer to have **more remorse, or more regrets**? I prefer more regrets. At least I have tried, I have followed my dreams. There is nothing worse than an existence lived in fear and ending in the remorse of not having followed our most important dreams. For most humans, the biggest dream is to achieve love happiness with a unique other person.

These **principles of how to achieve love happiness** (Tables 6,7) **should be thought in school**. Since day care, kindergarten, elementary school; after that, it's already too late. Love is like a foreign language. Some are naturally more inclined to learn it. All can master it with enough knowledge and practice.

The more you speak and practice love happiness, the better you'll become, the happier you and your partner will be. The bond of love is a living thing. If you don't attend to it, it withers. Speak it constantly, it's the most important language to learn.

There should also be a test for people thinking about having kids, a **test as a requirement to becoming parents**. So that we raise all kids to be secure lovers later as adults.

Strive to make your united life as a couple so positive as to radiate to our partner and really to all around you, to the world, beams of joy, of hope, like a diamond hit by a ray from the sun.

In a research study, happy-in-love couples ranked '**being best friends**' as the most important part of their relationship success. Altruistic love among equals is the recipe and the goal for romantic bliss.

Love gives the greatest sense of fulfillment. Success is making the most of who you are with what you have got. **Love is not a feeling; it is a way of behaving**. A behavior that shows your partner you care for their wellbeing, brings on the feeling of love. So usually it's behavior first, feeling second.

Then certainly the emotional feeling can drive further positive behavior, in an enchanted circle. A wonderful catch 22. It is not an easy catch 22. Doing something for others may not come easy, but it is rewarding. Love is the triumph of our joy of living a full positive life. Be nice, don't give up, don't leave, follow the principles (Tables 6,7).

Love is ultimately knowing and accepting ourselves; and knowing and accepting our partner. And giving without expecting sure reciprocation. It's a choice to be altruistic towards our partner, and just desire her happiness, the way she likes to be content.

What matters it's not just the differences between you and your partner, but even more how you handle them. The more you are secure in your attachment, similar in love languages, rich in the factors in tables 6 and 7, the more successful you'll be at achieving a lifetime of empathic love happiness.

For most of us, in our death beds, it's the quality of our connections with our loved ones, in particular with our one partner, that will matter most.

Hopefully my great grandkids will read this, and it will still be helpful for them. That's my dream.

When you finally find the person you want to spend the rest of your life with, you want the rest of your life to start as soon as possible.
In 'When Harry met Sally'

Tables

Table 1
Definition of love

- **Striving to help your partner be happy**

Table 2
<u>**Benefits of love**</u>

- For the individual
  - Better health
    - General
      - Eat healthier
      - More exercise
      - More frequent medical check-up and preventive medicine
      - More compliance with medical advice, and medication if needed
      - More energetic
      - More curious and engaged
      - Better concentration
      - More secure
      - Kinder, more caring
      - More positivity
      - More open, empathic to others
      - See others more positively
      - More attuned to others' emotions
      - More tolerant
      - More willing to engage with others
      - Increased mental health
      - More frequent sex
      - More pain tolerance
      - More independent (by being dependent on a stable partner)
      - Fewer discrepancies between their stated ideal and actual traits
      - Higher chance to achieve self-actualization (Figure 1)
    - Mood
      - Less stress

- Less anxiety
- Less depression
- Less post-traumatic stress disorder (PTSD)
- Less illicit substance use
- Less psychosis
- Less violence
- Less suicide
- Cardiac
  - Lower blood pressure
  - Decreased cardiac disease, including less coronary artery disease
  - Decreased death from heart disease
- Immune/Infections
  - Improved immune system
  - Reduced chance of getting infections
  - Less chance of getting sick
  - Less arthritis
- Cancer
  - Reduced change of getting cancer
  - Reduced death from cancer
- Longer life
- Higher level of Happiness
  - More positive attitude
  - More optimism
- Better financials
  - Better off money-wise
  - Pay less taxes and enjoy hundreds of federal perks (if married)[33]

- For the family
  - Increased chance of being a good parent
  - Happier kids

- For society

- Better, more creative workers
- More community builders
- More caring citizens
- Better leaders
- A more caring, altruistic world

Table 3
<u>**Attachment styles**</u>

- **Secure**
- **Anxious**
- **Avoidant**

Table 4
Attachment principles

- Find out what your attachment pattern is.[36,37]
- Acknowledge and accept your personal, unique, true attachment needs.
- Be your authentic self while dating and use effective communication. Talk about these attachment styles!
- Decide what attachment style in your partner is best for you.
- Learn to distinguish attachment patterns in others before you commit to friendship and/or relationship.
- If you are an anxious type, it's probably best to avoid avoidants.
- There are many superb individuals out there who have the attachment style to be superb partners for you.

Table 5
Love languages[4]

- **Physical touch**
- **Words of affirmation**
- **Acts of kindness**
- **Gifts**
- **Quality time**

Table 6
Essential Love Elements

- **Know who you are**
- **Partner open to love**
- **Courage**
- **They have to love you**
- **Altruism**
- **Positivity**
- **Trust**
- **Respect**
- **Forget a physical identikit**
- **Sexual intimacy**

Table 7
Factors associated with a successful long-term relationship

- Communication
- Emotional connection
- Commitment
- Fostering mutual admiration
- Be with someone who brings out the best in you
- Sharing goals
- Keeping passion
- Solve your solvable problems
- Accepting your partner: I love you despite
- Willingness to give up something
- Reasonable expectations
- Productive fighting

Table 8
VIA Classification of Character Strengths and Virtues[15]

- Wisdom and knowledge
  - Creativity
  - Curiosity
  - Judgement (thinking things through)
  - Love of learning
  - Perspective (people think of you as wise)
- Courage
  - Bravery
  - Honesty
  - Perseverance
  - Zest (approaching things with excitement and energy)
- Humanity
  - Kindness
  - Love (valuing close relationships with others)
  - Social intelligence (you know how to fit into different situations)
- Justice
  - Fairness (treating people fairly)
  - Leadership
  - Teamwork
- Temperance
  - Forgiveness
  - Humility
  - Prudence
  - Self-regulation
- Transcendence
  - Appreciation for beauty and excellence
  - Gratitude
  - Hope
  - Humor
  - Spirituality

Table 9
<u>Signs of failure</u>

- Failure to communicate
- Negativity
- Unwillingness to change
- Repetitive rejection
- Distracted outside the relationship (e.g. work, etc)
- Emotional connection is gone
- Multiple red flags
- Declines counseling
- Reasons to go
- Getting to despair
- Separation and Divorce

Table 10
<u>Reasons why you might want to quit your love relationship</u>[34]

- Never a time when things were good.
- Physical violence.
- Look at what you are doing, not at what you are saying.
- If somebody gave you permission, you would leave.
- There is not even one pleasure activity or interest you share (besides children).
- Your partner is not nice; he is not smart, he is neurotic, and he does not smell good.
- Your partner wants all the power.
- You feel humiliated and/or invisible in your relationship.
- Your partner does not let you talk about things that are important to you.
- Your partner lies.
- One of the partners does not like the other. No like, no love.
- You do not feel like you want to altruistically give to your partner anymore.
- You never touch each other.
- There is no person-specific sexual attraction.
- Your partner neither sees nor admits the very things you have been trying him to acknowledge as these make your relationship bad.
- Your partner admits to what you think is bad in the relationship, but he clearly is not willing to do anything about it.
- You just cannot let go of the vital problem you see in the relationship.
- You partner may be willing to change, but he is unable to change.
- Your partner crossed your personal bottom line.
- Your partner is different from you in a certain aspect, and you can't live with that.

- You consider the alternative to staying in your current relationship, and, looking at the real options, they are doable and a major improvement.
- Your partner makes you feel as a nut, or a jerk, or a loser, or an idiot.
- Your partner does not show clear concrete support for the things you are trying to do, the things that are important to you.
- You feel you will not lose something important if your relationship ends.
- There is a past hurt from your partner that you will never able to get over.
- Your partner is unable to forgive.
- You are unable as a couple to negotiate solutions when disagreements and problems arise.
- When you get close, your partner hurts you.
- You cannot get to intimacy with your partner.
- There is no more fun, or even hope for fun, in the relationship.
- You have no more shared goals and dreams with your partner.
- Even if all your relationship problems were solved today, you still feel ambivalent if to stay or leave.

Table 11
<u>Top reasons for divorce</u>[39]

- **Lack of emotional bond**
- **Infidelity or extramarital affair**
- **Balancing job and family**
- **Trouble with finances**
- **Lack of communication**
- **Constant arguing**
- **Weight gain**
- **Unrealistic expectations**
- **Lack of intimacy**
- **Lack of equality**
- **Not being prepared for marriage**
- **Physical or emotional abuse**

Table 12
Practical advice for long-term love happiness

- Love means wanting the other to be happy, their way. So love them that way.
- Be with someone who is like you in the things which matter the most to YOU.
- Be with someone who loves you back; and loves you back the way you like to be loved.
- Do not pretend for the other to change; this is a recipe for disaster.
- Focus on being happy yourself; discover what makes you happy.
- Spend over 1 hour together daily, or almost daily, one on one. Walks are best.
- Tolerate what you can tolerate.
- Do not tolerate what you think is impossible to tolerate for you to stay happy.
- Focus and borrow from other relationships you see as positive.
- Never give up on love. Stay positive. You'll be a better partner. For anyone out there.

Table 13
Selected sample signs of a positive empathic love relationship

1. Admit you're wrong after an argument
2. Say "I love you" before you go to sleep
3. Share household chores
4. Regular date nights, at least two a month, preferably weekly
5. Take turns to cook
6. Sex twice a week
7. Share the washing up
8. Same taste in films
9. Meet through mutual friends
10. Two shared hobbies
11. Share three mutual friends
12. Best friends
13. Kiss five times a day
14. Cuddle five times a day
15. Two romantic vacation breaks a year
16. Both work in some way
17. Have the same taste in food

Figure 1
Life Pyramid

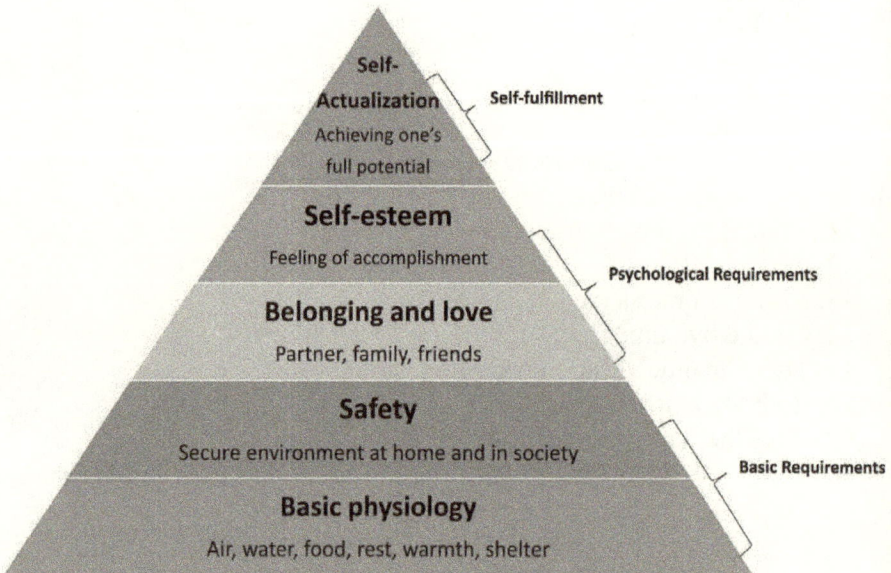

Figure 2
Trust to Emotional connection to Sex

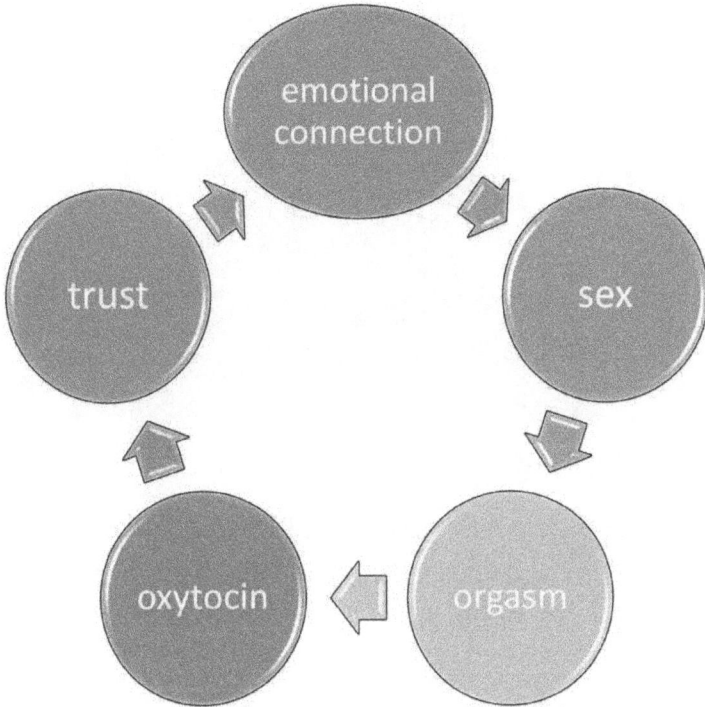

Figure 3
Pyramid of love

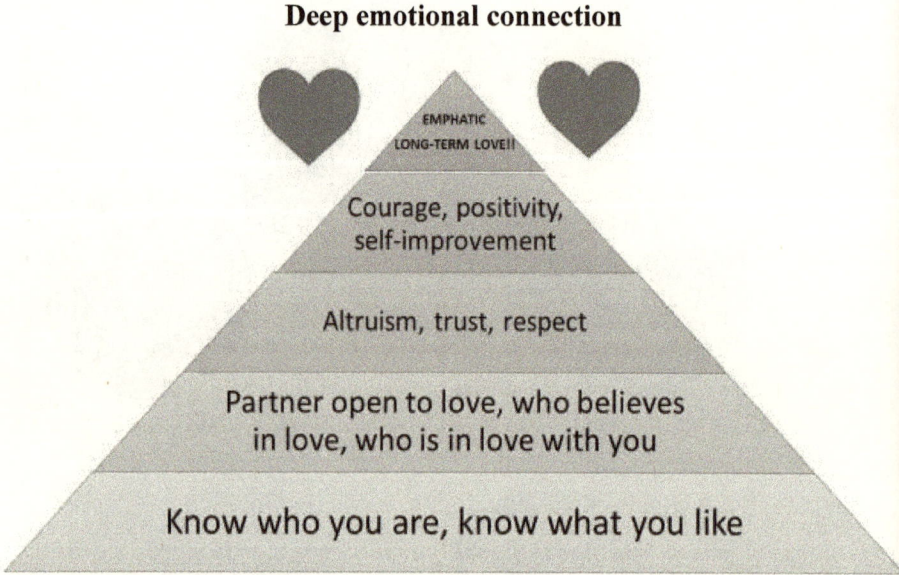

Deep emotional connection

EMPHATIC
LONG-TERM LOVE!!

Courage, positivity,
self-improvement

Altruism, trust, respect

Partner open to love, who believes
in love, who is in love with you

Know who you are, know what you like

References

1. Happiness: the scientific path to achieving well-being. Vincenzo Berghella.
   https://www.amazon.com/s?k=berghella+happiess&crid=1F4JOTK8CK09T&sprefix=berghella+happiess%2Caps%2C69&ref=nb_sb_noss
2. Dorothy Tennov. Love and Limerence. New Yor. Stein and Day. 1972. P 142.
3. Love Sense: The Revolutionary New Science of Romantic Relationships. Sue Johnson.
4. The 5 Love Languages: The Secret to Love that Lasts Paperback. Gary Chapman.
   https://5lovelanguages.com/quizzes/love-language
5. Me dentro: I primi scritti dai 17 ai 20 anni. Vincenzo Berghella.
6. Getting the Love You Want: A Guide for Couples. Harville Hendrix, Jack Garrett, et al.
7. The road less traveled. Scott Peck.
8. La vita a due. Willy Pasini.
9. Ying Chen, Maya B. Mathur, Brendan W. Case, Tyler J. VanderWeele. Marital transitions during earlier adulthood and subsequent health and well-being in mid- to late-life among female nurses: An outcome-wide analysis, Global Epidemiology, Volume 5, 2023, 100099,
10. ISSN 2590-1133, https://doi.org/10.1016/j.gloepi.2023.100099.
11. Horwitz TB, Balbona JV, Paulich KN, Keller MC. Evidence of correlations between human partners based on systematic reviews and meta-analyses of 22 traits and UK Biobank analysis of 133 traits. Nat Hum Behav. 2023 Aug 31. doi: 10.1038/s41562-023-01672-z. Epub ahead of print. PMID: 37653148.
12. Hold Me Tight: Seven Conversations for a Lifetime of Love. Sue Johnson, Helen Keeley, et al.
13. Men are from Mars, women are from Venus. John Gray.
14. https://store.gallup.com/p/en-us/10003/cliftonstrengths-34
15. VIA Institute of Character. www.viacharacter.org
16. Authentic Happiness: Using the New Positive Psychology to Realize Your Potential for Lasting Fulfillment. Martin E. P. Seligman.
17. Gottman JM, et al. (1998) Predicting marital happiness and stability from newlywed interactions. Journal of Marriage and the Family 60(1), 5-22.
18. Gottman JM (2001) The relationship cure. New York: Three Rivers press.
19. The How of Happiness: A Scientific Approach to Getting the Life You Want. Sonja Lyubomirsky.
20. Happy Together: Using the Science of Positive Psychology to Build Love That Lasts. Suzann Pileggi Pawelski and James O. Pawelski.
21. Lee BM et al. Communal Motivation and Well-Being in Interpersonal Relationships: An Integrative Review and Meta-Analysis. Psychological Bulletin 2018, Vol. 144, No. 1, 1–25
22. Give and Take: A Revolutionary Approach to Success. Adam M. Grant, Brian Keith Lewis, et al.
23. Fredrickson BL. (2009) Positivity: Top-notch research reveals the upward spiral that will change your life. New York. Three Rivers Press.
24. The Science of Trust: Emotional Attunement for Couples. John M. Gottman, J. Charles, et al.
25. https://apple.news/AX-kHbt8ZQvmy9jtqFxv47A
26. WHO data.
27. Rekindling desire. B and E McCarthy.
28. The Seven Principles for Making Marriage Work: A Practical Guide from the Country's Foremost Relationship Expert. John Gottman PhD and Nan Silver.
29. Savoring: a new model of positive experience. Bryant and Veroff.
30. From father to son. Vincenzo Berghella.
31. The Power of Moments: Why Certain Experiences Have Extraordinary Impact. Chip Heath and Dan Heath.

32. Reconcilable differences. Christensen, Doss, et al.
33. Overall NC, Fletcher GJO. Regulation Processes in Intimate Relationships: The Role of Ideal Standards. Journal of Personality and social psychology 2006;91:662-85.
34. Too good to go, too bad to stay. Kirshenbaum.
35. Anatomy of love: natural history of monogamy, of cheating and of divorce. Helen Fisher.
36. Attached: The New Science of Adult Attachment and How It Can Help You Find—and Keep—Love. Amir Levine, Rachel Heller, et al.
37. https://attachment.personaldevelopmentschool.com/quiz/?utm_source=google-search&utm_medium=cpc-lead&utm_campaign=18002521897&utm_term=&gc_id=18002521897&h_ad_id=63055570167 8&utm_content=personal%20development%20school%20attachment%20style%20quiz&gclid=E AIaIQobChMIqcj3l9rwgAMVi-_ICh1vNQ-3EAAYASAAEgLZovD_BwE
38. Austin Institute for The Study of Family and Culture
39. The case for marriage. Waite and Gallagher.

www.ingramcontent.com/pod-product-compliance
Lightning Source LLC
Chambersburg PA
CBHW031950080426
42735CB00007B/334